T.S. ELIOT'S CRITICAL ESSAYS : AN APPROACH FROM INDIAN AESTHETICS

T.S. Eliot's Critical Essays:
An Approach From
INDIAN AESTHETICS

Parthasarathi Mukhopadhyay

1993
Sharada Publishing House
DELHI-110052

First Published 1993

ISBN: 81-85616-14-0

Published by
B.L. BANSAL
for **SHARADA PUBLISHING HOUSE**
E-239, Shastri Nagar, Delhi-110052
Phone : 7516539

Laser Type setting by:
AKRITI COMPUTERS
B-5/98, Paschim Vihar, New Delhi-110063
Phone : 5584110, 5587403

Printed at:
GARG OFFSET WORK
B 76, Naraina Industria Area, New Delhi

To the sweet memory of revered grandfather Amitaranjan Mukherji – My Friend, Philosopher and Guide in teens – who opened before me the gates of the magnificent empire of learning – and inducted in me the habit of reading – with profound regards and affectionate admiration.

Contents

Preface 9
Conspectus 15
The Biography of T.S. Eliot 19

Chapter I
THE POET'S RELATIONS TO TRADITION 23
Section I -- Tradition -- What it is?
Section II -- Concept of Poet
Section III -- Tradition and Novelty

Chapter II
POET THE PERSON AND POET THE ARTIST 47
Section I -- Eliot's views on the Distinction
Section II -- Indian Aesthetics on the Issue
Section III -- Tagore on Distinction

Chapter III
THE MEANS OF COMMUNICATION 73
Section I -- Views of T.S. Eliot
Section II -- Stand of Indian Aesthetics
Section III -- Music and Meaning

Chapter IV
EXPRESSION AND ESCAPE – THE PARADOX OF 117
Section I -- Wordsworth and Eliot
Section II -- Indian Theory of Escape
Section III -- Synthesis

Chapter V
UTILITY OF POETRY 149
Section I -- Social Utility
Section II -- Absolute Utility

Chapter VI
RETROSPECT AND PROSPECT 159
Section I -- The Backward View
Section II -- Sri Aurobindo and the New Horizon
Bibliography 169

Preface

The book entitled *T.S. Eliot's Critical Essays : An Approach from Indian Aesthetics* records the results of long and laborious research carried out in the field of critical essays of T.S. Eliot vis-a-vis Sanskrit literary theories the results of which had been submitted earlier in the form of a thesis at Jadavpur University, Calcutta, in support of my candidature for admission to Ph. D. degree of the University. Now that the thesis has been approved by the University for award of Ph. D. degree, and that some of the adjudicators have suggested that the dissertation should be brought to light in order to enable the band of scholars working in the same field to advance the knowledge further by starting investigation from the truth substantiated in it, the book is being published with the co-operation of and the kind assistance rendered by Pandit Satkari Mukhopadhyaya in this regard and above all through the constant grace of the Divine Mother.

Professor Dr Jagannath Chakravorty, one of the most profound exponents of comparative criticism of the modern times, suggested to me the subject and explained its tremendous possibilities. Subsequently, he was pleased to agree to supervise the research project and guide me for Ph. D. degree of Jadavpur University. Unfortunately, Professor Chakravorty is no more to see the results of the research carried out under his supervision being published in the form of a book and to inspire me to undertake further projects. I happen to be the last research scholar to be guided by him, — last member to appear in 'the family of learning' (vidyavamsa) created by this great scholar, critic and literary artist. I offer my salutations soaked with devotion to Professor Chakravorty and seek his blessings in all my future ventures.

I had also the opportunity of discussing the contents of the thesis with Professor Dr Subhas Sarkar, Professor of English, Rabindra Bharati University, Calcutta, who happened to be one of the adjudicators and was pleased to conduct my Viva along with my supervisor. I am grateful of the very valuable suggestions offered by Professor Sarkar, a great exponent of Eliot's theory and Philosophy in regard to my future projects. The inspiration given by him is really tremendous and is likely to help me in carrying out new investigation in the field of practical application of the literary theories projected by T.S. Eliot to all specimens of poetic art including his own creations. This suggestion has been taken note of, and depending on the blessings of the Divine Mother and the spark of inspiration ignited by the learned connoisseur of T.S. Eliot, a start is contemplated to be given to the new scheme immediately after the publication of this book.

I had the privilege of going through some of the excerpts from the reports submitted by Dr Haydn Moore Williams on the thesis. The recommendations and remarks of Dr Williams have proved to me to be a source of a great strength, particularly because of the fact that Dr Williams happens to be a representative of both Western and Indian Cultures, — of the Western by his birth and of the Indian by his training and constant application to Indian texts and scriptures including the Gita, the Upanishads, the Vedas and the Puranas. The comments made by this learned scholar have been taken care of in the book. At this material moment, when the book is going to see the light of the day, I offer my profound respect to both Professor Dr Subhash Sarkar and Dr H.M. Williams for the kind words of encouragement, which they had been pleased to record in their reports.

The critical essays of T.S. Eliot occupy a pre-eminent position among world literature both by dint of vastness of their scope as also the fundamental nature of the problems tackled, — problems associated with creative as well as appreciative process of poetry. The present work makes a modest attempt to examine some of the fundamental problems related to creative and appreciative processes of poetry in the light of the solutions offered by the great literary artist-cum-critic T.S. Eliot and some profound literary critics belonging to the arena of Indian Aesthetics. It is astounding that there is profound similarity between the thought currents of T.S. Eliot and some of the noted literary critics of Indian scene, who inunciated principles relating to evaluation of poetry long back. Identification of these common points is likely to enable inquisitive readers to have a better idea of Eliot's philosophy of poetry as also to get a clear picture of the stand of Indian Aesthetics on these issues. The book entitled *T.S. Eliot's Critical Essay : An Approach from Indian Aesthetics* is divided into six chapters.

While the first chapter of the monograph discusses the place of tradition in the creative process of the literary artist and tries to tackle the problem as to whether it is necessary for the artist to know the mind of his own country, the second analyses the nature of the emotion experienced by the man who suffers and the mind which creates and shows how in the opinion of both T.S. Eliot and Abhinavagupta transmutation of raw feeling into emotion takes place in the mind of the literary artist. The third chapter tries to clarify the concept of 'Objective Correlative', as projected by Eliot and makes a modest attempt to establish its linkage with certain familiar concepts connected with the Rasa-Theory of Indian Aesthetics. The fourth chapter goes deep into the poetic process, and shows how it has been possible for Eliot to declare poetry as an escape from personality and not as an expression of personality. The identical approach of Indian Aesthetics is presented, and in course of this presentation, the chapter makes a reference to the distinction drawn by Tagore between 'Individuality' and 'Personality'. The fifth chapter presents the views of T.S. Eliot and Indian literary critics headed by Mammata on the utility of poetry, and in course of discussion of these views, it arrives at the conclusion that while social utility is a relative value, the repose of the being constitutes the absolute value. The last chapter takes a backward view of the total analysis and presents the findings arrived at in course of this research; at the same time, taking cue from the finding that poetry effects a transformation of the being, it moves into the arena of Sri Aurobindo's Aesthetics, and projects the viewpoint of Sri Aurobindo that future poetry is sure to assume the form of an incantation (mantra) and lead to spiritual rejuvenation and enlightenment.

My father Professor Dr Debranjan Mukherji of the University of Burdwan and my uncle Professor Dr Ramaranjan Mukherji, one of the accepted authorities in Indian Literary Theories initiated me into the hieroglyphics of Sanskrit Texts on literary criticism. In beds, in dining tables, in course of travels and walks my uncle reminded me of the complex theories of literary criticism, both occident and orient, and all the while guided to complete my project without which, it is sure, the work would not have seen the light of the day.

'My heart aches and a drowsy numbness pains my sense' while remembering my late grandfather Amitaranjan Mukherji for whom only I could venture to step into the field of Humanities in my secondary level and practically it was my grandfather who, with his affectionate cover, did light the lamp to find my way in the vast arena of Humanities stream in my earlier days of childhood. On the verge of submission of my dissertation I feel his presence around myself, and solicit his affectionate blessings.

While my mother Sm. Namita Devi blessed me and my wife Sm. Aparna Mukherji invoked the blessings of the Divine Mother for the successful completion of the project as well as occasionally reminded me of the time-limit, prompting me to finish the work within the scheduled period, my aunt Dr Arati Mukherji of Rabindra Bharati University did throw very valuable suggestions on my problems of discussion at every step of my work. With deep humility and profound gratitude I acknowledge the contributions of all to the making of my dissertation. I will be failing in my duty if I do not mention the name of my elder sister Sm. Malabika Sarkar, the affections of whom know no bounds. With motherly care and affection she did nurture me at every step. My nephew Surjyadeep did place me first on a little higher position in the family after his birth in 1979 and his childish enquiries about my project did certainly strengthen my mind in the midst of routine works. My brother-in-law Sri Siddhartha Sarkar, with his natural smiling temperament, had often enquired of the progress of my thesis. My second nephew Rajdeep's enchanting prattling also renewed my energy to a great extent.

I am extremely thankful to Dr Amarnath Bhattacharyaya of the Department of Philosophy, University of Burdwan, who has wide spectrum of experience, for very kindly rendering all assistance to me in making the dissertation as beautiful as possible and also to Dr Manabendu Banerji and Professor Bhabaniprasad Bhattacharyya, both of the Department of Sanskrit, Jadavpur University for tendering frequent advice to me on technical matters.

I put on record my words of appreciation for the constant advice tendered to me by my revered teachers Sri Madhusudan Pramanik of SIURI Benimadhab Institution and Sri Mohinimohan Mukherji of Siuri. My words also fail to express my indebtedness to my University teachers-- Dr S.L. Bhattacharyya, Dr S.R. Banerji, Dr D.K. Barua, Dr Mrs. R. Kundu, Dr M.K. Sen, Prof. L.N. Gupta, Dr M.K. Roy, Dr Mrs. A. Biswas, Prof. Sadananda Chakraborty -- all of the Department of English, University of Burdwan, without whose constant blessings and inspirations it would not have been possible for me to undertake the project.

I had the good fortune of receiving encouragement from my friends and colleagues and I shall be failing in my duty if I do not make special mention of some of them. Dr Sudhir Roy, M.P. and former President, Governing Body of my College and Dr Jimutabahan Bhattacharyya, Principal, Birbhum Mahavidyalaya extended all assistance to me all the while and all my colleagues did provide a congenial working atmosphere in the College, enabling me to devote my total energy to Research. My sincere thanks are due to all of them.

Successful completion of a project, however, does not

depend only on the pleasant atmosphere in the place of work, but also on congenial atmosphere at home. This was provided to me by all the members of the family and the inmates of the house, namely Anandagopal Roy, Dulal Chandra Chatterji, Debaprasad Banerji, Samiran Roy, Debkumar Chatterji, Madanmohan Thakur, Tapan Kumar Chatterji, Rajendra Giri, Tapan Naskar, Ajit Kumar Ghosh and others. Sri Baniprasad Banerji of SIURI rendered yeoman's service to me regarding preparation of manuscript whenever needed. Dr Swami Mahananda of Abhedananda Mahavidyalaya, Sainthia always discussed with me the points of my dissertation with affectionate care. In the last phase of the work a lovely breeze of freshness pervaded the house and the family with the birth of my son, the little Subhadeep (Devilal), the first representative of the next generation making the atmosphere more pleasant. I am, therefore, bound by a debt of gratitude to all of them.

Last but not the least I have to make a special mention of the untiring efforts made by Sri Jamini Ganguly in making the typescript of the dissertation within a short time so that the time-schedule prepared earlier could be maintained.

I invoke finally the blessings of the Divine Mother and release the book, my first offering to the altar of the Goddess of Learning, to the land of the academic community for consideration.

Siuri Kalilari,
Amitaranjan Sarani,
Siuri, Birbhum — Parthasarathi Mukhopadhyay
Kalipuja, 1399 B.S.

October 25, 1992

Conspectus

The Critical Essays of T.S. Eliot occupy a pre-eminent position among World Literature both by dint of vastness of their scope and the nature of problems tackled — problems associated with creative as well as appreciate process of Poetry. The objective of the present dissertation is to take a few selected observations of Eliot, — to examine the problems intended to be projected, and to present the reaction of Indian Aesthetics to the problems as also to the solutions proposed by Eliot. It is astounding that there is profound similarity between thought-currents of T.S. Eliot and some of the noted literary critics of Indian scene, who enunciated principles of evaluation of poetry long back. Identification of these common points will enable inquisitive readers to have a better idea of Eliot's Philosophy of Poetry as also of the approach of Indian Aesthetics to some of the fundamental problems relating to the genesis of Art Form in Poetry.

As it is not possible to discuss all the problems raised by Eliot in the small span of a single dissertation. The present monograph takes up the observations of Eliot listed below and structures his philosophy of Poetry on the basis of these and also projects at the same time the views of Indian Literary Criticism on the problems.

1. 'No Poet, no artist of any art, has his complete meaning alone. His significance, his appreciation is the appreciation of his relation to the dead poets and artists. .... He must be aware of the mind of his own country -- a mind which he learns in time to be much more important than his own private mind.'

When Sanskrit Poetics tenders advice to Poets to make themselves acquainted with the Creations of master artists and speaks of the necessity of honouring 'Tradition' they refer possibly to the same thing.

> 2. 'The more perfect the artist, the more completely separate in him will be the man who suffers and the mind which creates.'

When Anandavardhana describes the first specimen of Poetic Art as an external manifestation of the tragic emotion, and Abhinavagupta draws the line of demarcation between actual grief experienced by the sage and transmutation of that feeling into emotion in the mind of the literary artist, they refer to the same process.

> 3. 'The only way of expressing emotion in the form of art is by finding an 'objective correlative', in other words, a set of objects, a situation, a chain of events, which shall be the formula of that particular emotion; such that when the external factors, which must terminate in sensory experience, are given, the emotion is immediately evoked.'

When Bharata enunciates the famous aphorism relating to attainment of Poetic Experience, and says that *Rasa* is brought to a relishable state through combination of the permanent moods with excitants, situations, ensuents and accessories, does he give expression to the same theory? An analysis of the process of the Poetic Experience, as given by later theoreticians is in a position to throw more light on the problem.

> 4. 'Poetry is not a turning loose of emotion, but an escape from emotion; it is not the expression of personality, but an escape from personality.'

Sanskrit Poetics admits the process of 'universalisation' and says that it operates in two areas; in the area of the subject as also in the area of the object, and in both the processes of creation and appreciation of Poetry. Proper explanation of the concepts of 'hrdayasamvada', 'tanmayibhava', and 'sadharanikarana' is likely to be of great help in understanding the concept of 'escape from personality'.'

5. 'Every Poetry would like, I fancy, to be able to think that he had some direct social utility.'

Sanskrit Poetics expends its energies in analysing the benefits that are supposed to accrue from Poetry, and in course of this analysis it makes mention of moral values, ethical standards and liberation implying thereby that Poetry has something to do with morals and religion.

After identifying the similarities in the thought-currents of T.S. Eliot and some of the literary critics belonging to the Indian scene on the problems identified, the thesis makes a modest attempt to take a flight into the arena of Sri Aurobindo that future poetry is to take the form of a mantra, and to lead to spiritual upliftment.

The dissertation thus is intended to present an analysis of the viewpoints of T.S. Eliot on some fundamental problems connected with poetry, – its creative process and appreciation by applying the principles formulated in Indian Aesthetics.

THE BIOGRAPHY OF T.S. ELIOT

Chronologically Arranged

1888	:	Born St. Louis Missouri, 26 September.
1896	:	His father builds summer residence in Gloucester, Massachusetts.
1898	:	Attends Smith Academy, St. Louis, Until 1905.
1905	:	First poems published in Smith Academy Record. Attends Milton Academy, near Boston.
1906	:	Begins studies at Harvard.
1908	:	Read Arthus Symons's The Symbolist Movement in Literature (1899).
1909	:	Graduates A.B.
1910	:	Graduates A.M. In his time at Harvard, various poems published in Harvard, Advocate
1910-1911	:	Residence in Paris: attends Bergson's Lectures. Visits Munich.
1911	:	Studies Philosophy at Harvard until 1914.
1914	:	Visits Paris and Marburg. In August goes to Merton College, Oxford, to continue philosophical studies. Meets Ezra Pound in London.

1915	:	Marries Vivien Haigh-Wood. Teaches at High Sycombe Grammar School. First British publication, 'Preludes' and 'Rhapsody on a Windy Night' in Blast.
1916	:	Teaches at Highgate Junior School. Completes thesis.
1917	:	Works at Lloyds Bank. Assistant editor of The Egoist Prufrock and other Observations and Ezra Pound – his Metric and Poetry published.
1919	:	Father dies. Poems, 'Tradition and the Individual Talent', 'Hamlet' published.
1920	:	Are vus [sic] Prec and The Sacred Wood published.
1921	:	Ill. Recovers at Margate and Lausanne. Drafts The Waste Land. 'The Metaphysical Poets' published. Mother visits London.
1922	:	The Waste Land published in the first issue of The Criterion and also in book form in USA.
1923	:	The Waste Land published in book form in England.
1925	:	Joins Faber and Gwyer. Poems 1909-1925 published.
1926	:	Gives Clark Lectures at Cambridge.
1927	:	Received in Chruch of England. 'Journey of the Magi' published. Becomes British Citizen.

1928	:	A Song for Simeon and For Lancelot Andrews Published.
1929	:	'Dante' and 'Animula' published.
1930	:	Ash-Wednesday and Marina published.
1931	:	Thoughts after Lambeth and 'Triumphat March' published.
1932	:	Selected Essays 1917-1932. Charles Eliot Norton Professor of Poetry at Harvard. Gives Page-Barber Lectures at University of Virginia. 'Sweency Agonistes'.
1933	:	Legal separation from Vivien Eliot.
1934	:	The Rock first performed and published. After Strange Gods published. Visits Burnt Norton.
1935	:	Murder in the Cathedral first performed and published.
1936	:	Collected Poems 1909-1935 (includes 'Burnt Norton'), and Modern published.
1937	:	Visits East Coker.
1939	:	The Family Reunion first performed and published. Old Possum's Book of Practical Cats. Last issue of The Christian. The Idea of a Christian Society published.
1940	:	'East Coker' published. Fire-watcher during German bombing of London.

1941	:	'The Dry Salvages' published.
1942	:	'Little Gidding' published.
1943	:	Four Quartets published complete.
1945	:	What is a Classic? published. Visits Ezra Pound in hospital.
1947	:	Honorary Degree from Harvard University. Death of Vivien Eliot.
1948	:	Order of Merit. Nobel Prize for Literature. Notes towards the Definition of Culture published.
1949	:	The Cocktail Party first performed; Published in 1950.
1951	:	Poetry and Drama Published.
1953	:	The Confidential Clerk first performed Published in 1954.
1954	:	Receives Hanseatic Goethe Prize.
1957	:	Marries Valerie Fletcher. On Poetry and Poets published.
1958	:	The Elder Stateman first performed and published.
1963	:	Collected poems 1909-1962 published. US Medal of Freedom.
1964	:	Knowledge and Experience in the philosophy of F.H. Bradley.
1965	:	Dies London 4 January. Ashes interred at East Coker in April.
1969	:	Complete Poems and Plays (one vol.) published.

CHAPTER I

The Poet's Relations to Tradition

Section I

Tradition — What it is?

Eliot's contribution to the stock of critical essays is not only sizeable, but from the standpoint of quality also it occupies the highest position. These critical essays present on the one hand, literary principles obtained through accumulated experience, and at the same time project certain norms of adjudication which help the connoisseur to evaluate the poet and his literary art. Gifted with profound Imagination and Critical Acumen, Eliot dives deep into the mind of the literary artist, as the creative process starts operating in him, and brings out the different stages in the process of creation of poetry successfully, so much so that, his analysis reaches at times the precision of Science. This scientific approach and technique of investigation applied to the arena of Art imparts to his Critical Essays a scientific temper, which is not traceable in writings of many critics of the occident and orient. The way of Eliot's exposition is different from that of his predecessors. He is more of an Aristotelian than a Platonist. His analytical approach reminds one of Coleridge minus the latter's romantic exuberance.

The Biography of T.S. Eliot shows that this great poet-cum-critic had the opportunity of studying the Upanishads and the Gita during his studentship at Cambridge and the peculiar trait of ancient Indian literature had cast so tremendous influence on his poetic personality that he could absorb within him the Indian spirit and give expression to some of the peculiar traits of this mind in a novel way, making the principle of literary criticism applicable to contemporary literature and bearing relevance to all types of literature of all ages. This enchantment of Eliot for Indian Philosophy and ancient Indian Literature explains the amazing similarity between the thought-current projected by him in some of his critical essays and the thought-current floated by Indian Aesthetics in selected areas. This similarity is so amazing that, an intelligent interpretation of critical essays, written by noted Indian Literary Critics becomes absolutely necessary for understanding Eliot's Philosophy of Poetry and Literary Art. It often seems that without having an idea of the principle formulated by Indian Aesthetics, it is not possible to enter into the mystery of Eliot's critical essays, that are characterised by profundity of thought.

In his essay entitled *Tradition and the Individual Talent,* T.S. Eliot introduces the concept of Tradition and tries to give an intelligent exposition of the relation which a Poet is expected to bear to Tradition. In this essay he refutes the contention of Wordsworth that, Poetry takes its origin in emotion recollected in tranquility, and that it is an expression of the personality of the poet. The novel idea of the process of 'depersonalization' of the poet, as the creative process starts operating in him is projected for the first time in Western Criticism: but this concept of 'depersonalization' forms the sheet-anchor of Indian Aesthetics, and consequently, this enquiry into amazing similarity of thought-currents can start with this concept of 'depersonalization', which is intimately linked with the concept of Tradition.

'Tradition' usually is taken to mean the body of customs or beliefs handed down from ancestors to posterity: it also refers to the literary principle or any other theories obtained through accumulated experience, — the experience, not of persons, but of the nation as a whole. Eliot discourages adherence to Tradition for the literary artists, because tradition usually refers to blind adherence to the beliefs and customs handed down to posterity. This Tradition, which according to Eliot, is the degenerated form of Tradition, consists in following the ways of immediate generation, — of moving in the beaten track followed by the ancestors, and consequently is to be avoided at all costs. It is for this reason that the word 'traditional' is applied as a phrase of censure, and when a specimen of Poetic Art is declared as 'traditional', what is meant is that, the literary artist in the present case is incapable of presenting new thoughts and adopt fresh techniques that can strike the mind of the connoisseur as having enchantment of their own. This Tradition, which is nothing but blind adherence to set beliefs and customs and techniques handed down from ancestors to posterity is definitely to be avoided.

To T.S. Eliot, however, 'Tradition' is a matter of much wider significance. To Eliot, Tradition is not timid adherence to beliefs and/or customs or techniques introduced by immediately preceding generation, but it is a historical sense, involving a clear perception of the past. This historical sense consists in the knowledge relating to the mind of the nation, — the mind of the poets preceding the literary artists themselves, beginning from the literary artists, who wrote in the morning of mankind down to the artists who immediately preceded the present literary artist himself. This Tradition which is but another name of historical sense consists, therefore, in the knowledge of the element of present shining for all time to come in the womb of the past. Past incidents and events change: they lose their grace and enchantment with passage of time, but the element of present remaining latent in the past continues for all time to come, making it possible for the appreciative readers of new generation to appreciate the works of literary art composed long back. To acquire this historical sense, — to locate the elements permanently present in the womb of the past is, according to Eliot, to follow the Tradition. This tradition is not blind adherence to the beliefs and techniques handed down by ancestors, but a vivid perception of the past, which shows that there is an element of present in even the remote past.

In expounding the concept of 'Historical Sense', T.S. Eliot proceeds to say that this does not refer to an idea derived through acquaintance with historical works, since historical works only give an analysis of the events from the point of view of the historian; it refers rather to the sense of the timeless, as well as the temporal and of the timeless and temporal together. The incidents and facts of life happen in the background of time and, consequently, they are temporal. The permanent feelings experienced by the characters participating in the facts of life and incidents continue for all time to come, and consequently they are timeless. 'Tradition', according to T.S. Eliot, consists in this historical sense, which is nothing other than a sense of the timeless and temporal taken together, — a sense of the permanent feelings and inclinations and dispositions, as also of the changing situations and incidents, that are bound to occur in the realm of reality. To adhere to Tradition, thus, as Eliot thinks, is not to adhere blindly to the customs and techniques introduced by artists of past generations, but to surrender to the timeless elements of the past, the elements which shine in their undeemed splendour for all time to come. It is this projection of the timeless that makes the literary artist great and enables the documents of literary art to preserve its enchantment for all time to come.[1]

Indian Aesthetics does not make an analysis of Tradition in the context of its relation to the Poet, in the manner it is done by Eliot, but it makes copious reference to Tradition in the context of genesis of Poetry, making it possible to locate Indian concept of Tradition in the area of literary art. Tradition or Parampara, Indian theory says, is a bundle of thoughts and instructions obtained from accumulated experience and handed down from generation to generation since the early morning of mankind. In order to have a proper idea of this *Tradition* it is necessary to analyse the observations of Indian Aesthetics in the context of genesis of poetry and selection of themes.

In its endeavour to present the equipments that are necessary for creation of Poetry Indian Aesthetics refers to Imagination, dexterity acquired through acquaintance with compositions of master-minds and all the branches of learning and constant practice to compose Poetry under the guidance of experts in the art and science of Poetry as conjointly constituting the causal factor of Poetic Creation, implying thereby, that it is necessary to make oneself acquainted with the creation of the master-minds before laying his hands upon creation of Poetry.[2] The mind of the nation flows through the writings of all master-artists, and to know the composition of master-artists with an open mind is to know the mind of the nation, — to catch the trend of the nation as a whole, so that the trend can be followed and supplemented further by artists of new generations. In a different context, Indian Aesthetics tenders advice to Poets of posterity to choose themes of their creations from the classics and standard works of literature, the dominant emotional mood of which is well-known, so that the entire nation can take part in the intellectual and spiritual feast expected to be thrown by the document of literary art, going to be produced by the artist. Anandavardhana, the brilliant expounder of the doctrine of Dhvani advises Poets of posterity to draw themes of their works from writings, the emotional content of which is familiar and fixed, — the peculiar name given to such compositions being 'siddharasa' and says that when the new literary artist composes poems by adhering to the mind of the *nation*, i.e. samaja or people — by incorporating the permanent feelings or melodies appreciated by the nation, it becomes possible for him to produce Grand Poetry, that is capable of preserving its enchantment for all time to come.[3]

Indian Aesthetics realises the danger of introducing innovation of all types, both in the area of selection of themes and selection of techniques, because new things running contrary to the mind of the *nation* may appear unattractive to the connoisseur and new techniques may prove shocking to him and stand in the way of attainment of poetic experience, technically known as 'Rasasvada' in the terminology of the Sanskrit Poetics. This does not however, mean that the poet is to narrate the same old stories and adopt the same techniques adopted by earlier Poets, because this narration and adoption is likely to make Poetry stale and unattractive. What is meant is that the permanent emotive contents are to be taken note of and new super-structures are to be constructed on the solid rock of these permanent moods, so that the specimens of literary arts produced can retain their beauty and shiningness for all time to come. Anandavardhana makes it clear that, the facts of life presented long back by literary artists of hoary past can be handled successfully by the literary artists of today, provided they are in a position to present successfully the excitants, the ensuents, and the permanent moods necessary for depiction of emotional moods (Rasa). Anandavardhana declares that when a specimen of Literary Art becomes successful in presenting emotional mood, and when this mood absorbs the total consciousness of the appreciators, then even an old theme handled by the poet appears fresh and charming : once again it inspires the readers by its greatness and sublimity. In his endeavour to press this point home, Anandavardhana draws the parallelism of the trees acquiring freshness in spring, and says that just as the vigour of the spring imparts freshness to the old trees, which shine once again in their rich foliage, similarly the brilliant technique of the literary artist in presenting the emotional mood inducts freshness to the old themes and incidents.[4] When Anandavardhana makes this declaration, what he means is that the literary artist is to make himself acquainted with the permanent moods and emotions, — the likes and dislikes, — the inclinations and aspirations, not only of one individual or a group of individuals, but of the nation or community, as a whole. This concept of Anandavardhana finds a close similarity to the concept of historical sense projected by T.S. Eliot under the umbrella of 'Tradition'.

Tagore gives a beautiful exposition of this theme in his memorable poem *Puraskar*. In this poem Tagore says that incidents and facts of life may come and go, but the feelings which give rise to these happenings or the impact which these incidents produce in the mind continue for all time to come, filling the minds of new generations with their fragrance. The bloody battle that took place between the Kauravas and the Pandavas has become a thing of the past, — and so is the banishment of Sita, — but the attitudes that gave rise to these incidents and the impacts which they created in the minds of men continue for all time making it possible to identify the mind of the Nation.[5] And when the question of locating the mind of Indian Nation comes, one is naturally required to take into account the profundity of thoughts presented in the Vedas, the Upanishads and the Classics to read which an advice has been tendered constantly by the Indian Aesthetics, particularly to Poets aspiring after greatness.

Section II

Concept of Poet

T.S. Eliot describes the mind of the poet as a shred of platinum in his endeavour to put forward a parallelism in regard to a catalyst. It is said that when two gases are mixed in the presence of a filament of platinum they form sulphurous acid. This combination takes place in the presence of the platinum; but neither the two gases contain any trace of platinum nor is the platinum affected by such combination. Similarly T.S. Eliot thinks, in order to constitute poetic emotion, which resides in Poetry rather than in the individual Poet, it is necessary for the poetic mind to exist; but nevertheless neither the mind of the individual poet is affected by the poetic emotion nor does the new emotion taking shape contains any trace of the sensibility of the individual mind of the Poet. This assertion of T.S. Eliot brings into light his conviction that the emotion presented in Poetry is distinct from the emotion experienced by the individual Poet, and that a special faculty of the poetic mind is necessary to effect transmutation of the ordinary feeling into an extraordinary poetic emotion.

Though in his critical essay entitled *Tradition and the*

Individual Talent Eliot does not give an analysis of the special feature of the poetic mind or the equipments necessary for the literary artist, in another critical essay entitled *Metaphysical Poets* he gives an analysis of the poet's mind when it starts operating. When a poet's mind is perfectly equipped for this work, Eliot says, it constantly amalgamates desparate experience and it is on this point that, it differs from the experience of the ordinary man. The ordinary man's experience is chaotic, irregular and fragmentary, while the experience of the poet is always complete, inasmuch as, a number of reactions created in the poetic mind are combined into wholes in his experience. The experience of the ordinary man thus takes note of fragments and parts, while experience of the poet takes notice of wholes and brings into being absolute totalities, marked by homogeneity and grandeur of the Great.[6]

Though T.S. Eliot does not make any mention of the special equipment of the Poet, which lies behind the transformation of the ordinary into the extra-ordinary or the genesis of the complete whole by combining together fragmentary experiences, it is perfectly clear that, a particular equipment is an absolute necessity, and that this equipment is capable of being represented by Intellect or Imagination, by whatever name it may be called. In this connexion, it may be profitable to analyse the viewpoints of some of the literary critics of Nineteenth Century, who must have exerted some influence at least on Eliot. In his essay entitled *The Hero as Poet* Thomas Carlyle refers to the seeing eye of the poet and hastens to suggest that this seeing eye discloses the inner harmony of things, — what nature means, what musical idea nature wraps up in seemingly rough embodiments. Continuing his proposition that the "seeing eye" is an essential equipment of the literary artist, Carlyle proceeds to say that, to the poet as to every other, what is essential is vision, — the gift of eye. If the poet is unable to see, it is of no use to keep stringing rhymes together, jingling sensibilities against each other and name himself a poet. Carlyle thinks that this "seeing" eye" is nothing other than Intellect, and the other faculties like Imagination, Fancy, etc. which are much in discussion, are capable of being comprehended under this great faculty of Intellect. In giving a critical account of Shakespeare, therefore, Carlyle remains satisfied by saying that Shakespeare is the greatest of Intellects; he feels that this statement is in a position to express all the accomplishments of this great Dramatist.[7]

Though Carlyle refuses to give Imagination, Fancy and such other instruments their due share, other literary critics, writing immediately before T.S. Eliot prefer to give all these faculties their due weightage. Expounding the applicability of Carlyle's theory of Truth in the context of poetry, Leigh Hunt says that, truth of every kind belongs to the Poet, provided it can bud into any kind of beauty or is capable of being illustrated and impressed by the poetic faculty of Imagination. It is the faculty of Imagination which converts the ordinary truth into poetic truth and presents it as steeped in fathomless beauty. Hunt extends recognition to seven different kinds and degrees of Imagination, some of which are necessary for formation of every true poet, and all of which are necessary for formation of the great literary artist. The first degree of Imagination presents to the mind any object or circumstance in every-day life as steeped in beauty. The second degree presents the real, but not every-day circumstance; but the real also acquires enchantment by a touch of the poetic faculty. The third degree of Imagination combines characters and events directly imitated from a real life with imitative realities of its own invention; characters and events thus imitated, however, acquire new dimensions. The fourth degree of Imagination conjures up things and events not to be found in nature: it creates totally new things and worlds. The fifth degree of Imagination is that, which in order to illustrate or aggravate one image, introduces another, sometimes through simile, sometimes through metaphor and sometimes through certain other poetic figures. The sixth degree of Imagination reverses this process and makes a variety of circumstances taking different colours from different perceptions. The seventh degree, which represents the highest one surpasses in its effect the extremest force of the most particular description, so much so, that the profound beauty of the new transmuted description is impressed in the mind of the reader in no time. Drawing the line of distinction between Imagination and Fancy, Hunt says that Fancy is the younger sister of Imagination without the other's weight of thought and feeling. When analysed, Imagination may dissolve into feeling, — the feeling of the subtlest type, — the perception of sympathies in the nature of things or in their popular contribution. Fancy is more or less superlative in nature: it loves to toy with airy and fantastical creations. Imagination, thus, is strong, sympathetic and responsible; fancy is weak, frivolous and irresponsible. It is possibly for this reason that Hunt allocates the sorrows in the field of Targedy to Imagination and the frivolous field of the Comic to Fancy.[8] All these speculations of Western Aesthetics, including those of T.S. Eliot show that for creation of Poetical Paintings a faculty of the poetic mind is necessary; this faculty enables the literary artists to see things in their proper perspectives, – their essential and real nature, as distinct from the ordinary ones, – as a complete whole having homogeneity and at the same time to curve out images, that may prove themselves as strong citadels of poetic emotion.

T.S. Eliot is not the only critic to describe the experience of the poet as 'always forming new wholes'. When T.S.Eliot propounds the theory that, while the ordinary man's experience is chaotic and fragmentary, the experience of the literary artist is homogenious and a complete whole, he gives expression to a profound truth which is capable of being located after a clear analysis of the entire creative process. It is interesting to note that literary critics in the area of Indian Aesthetics also try to go deep into the mystery of the creative process, and in course of their search they arrive at almost identical propositions. Indian theory conceives of the poet as primarily "a seer of Truth",– as a gifted person to whom the poetic truth reveals itself in its full splendour. When this sense is taken into account, the Sanskrit term "Kavi" becomes a synonym of the expression "risi", inasmuch as, the primary function of the really gifted chosen man is to see the truth. It is not without reason, therefore, that the entire Vedic literature refers to the literary artists as "risis", implying thereby that a set of verified and verifiable truth revealed themselves to these artists. This statement itself rules out the animadversion of the critics of the Vedas that, these do not reflect truths, but rather project certain thoughts, which do not have any correspondence to reality.

The statement that literary artists are seers of truth signifies deeper meanings, and it is not that simple as it appears to be. Indian mind conceives of Truth as a complete whole, and asserts that while completeness leads to beauty, fragmentariness leads to ugliness. And the Absolute, which represents a combination of Truth and Beauty is always an indivisible whole. When therefore the Vedas envisage a literary artist a the seer of Truth, it acknowledges the existence in the artist of a capacity to realise the unfragmented truth and form his ordinary experiences into a complete whole, so that the unfragmented truth in totality can be reflected in poetical paintings, curved out by him.

It is interesting that literary theoreticians of later period conceive of the literary artist as one gifted with two faculties, - the faculty of realising the truth, which naturally is an unfragmented whole, and the faculty of curving out poetical paintings competent to give expression to the total truth. Indian theory at its later stage of development, thus, combines the faculty of constructing poetic images with the faculty of experiencing total truth, and makes the literary artist more gifted than the literary artist, conceived of in the Vedas.

The assertion of Eliot that the experiences occurring in the mind of the poet are always forming new wholes naturally envisages the existence of a powerful imagination in the artist, because it is this faculty alone which is in a position to effect synthesis between fragmented experiences and present a beautiful whole. The statement of Indian literary theory that the poet is a seer of grand truth also invites the literary artist with this faculty of Imagination, which presents ever fresh beauties to the artist and enables him to discover the indivisible whole in fragmented experiences, – the seat of the most beautiful in the most deformed. It is equally interesting that Abhinavagupta, the learned commentator of *Dhvanyaloka* describes Imagination as the faculty of creating splendidly beautiful words and paintings, and in giving an analysis of this faculty existing in the literary artists, he says that, it consists in the power to create poetry surcharged with profundity of emotion, – a power that lies latent in the mind of the artist experiencing an afflux of significant emotion (Rasa). The employment of the expression 'Rasa' itself goes to indicate the indivisible and total experience of the literary artist, inasmuch as, Rasa is experienced not in the midst of disintegrated ideas and disjoined images, but in the midst of integrated experience, and connected ideas. When Indian literary theory, thus, predicates the existence of *rasa* with reference to the mind of the literary artist, it naturally affirms the theory that, at the time of creation of poetry, the artist derives complete and integrated experience, as a result of which it becomes possible for him to construct integrated images and project the total theme therethrough.

The question whether *rasa* belongs to the literary artist or to the refined appreciator or to the poem as a whole may raise its head at this material moment, and may give rise to certain confusions, because the appreciative connoisseur is usually believed to experience *rasa*. It is, however, to be noted that the expression *rasa* as employed in Indian theory has got a wide semantic spectrum, and it is employed not only in relation to the connoisseur, but in relation to the literary artist and the whole poem also. Anandavardhana and Abhinavagupta refuse to accept the proposition that, the literary artist does not experience *rasa* or significant emotion, because, as both of them affirm, how can the artist communicate the exalted emotion unless it is experienced by him. The statement made in Indian theory that the literary artist experiences ordinary emotions, while the refined connoisseur savours the delight of significant emotion, technically known as *rasa* has naturally led to certain confusions, but it is to be remembered that Indian theory has always maintained the distinction between ordinary emotion and exalted emotion, as also between the mind of the poet in his individual capacity and the mind of the poet in his universal capacity. A difference, thus, is to be made between the experiencing mind of the artist in his individual capacity and the experiencing mind of the poet in its universal creative capacity. Indian theory draws this line of demarcation with meticulous care, reminding one of the distinction drawn by Eliot between "the man who suffers and the mind which creates". A detailed chapter is intended to be devoted to this study, and hence it is not elaborated here.

In describing the role of Imagination Indian literary theory states that this faculty creates new entities and worlds which are not experienced in the ordinary world, – presents ever-fresh flashes of beauty and enables the artists to construct homogeneous and complete poetical paintings. Without expounding the details of this imagination in its myriad aspects Mammata explains it as the germ of poetry, and expounding this doctrine says that, without it poetry is not produced and if produced at all, it makes the specimen of poetic art an object of ridicule. The small statement that imagination constitutes the chief causal factor of poetry is surcharged with profound truth, inasmuch as, it presents the extremely significant role played by imagination in genesis of poetry. For creation of poetry the literary artist is required to derive an individual experience, – to convert this individual experience into a universal experience, – to connect the fragmentary experience into a complete whole, – to open the gateway of a new Art-world, – and finally to identify the poetic texture competent to give expression to this splendidly charming total indivisible experience. Mammata proclaims that all the actions required to be performed by the literary artists are done with the assistance of this strong faculty of Imagination, which is regarded as the first equipment necessary for the literary artist. Theoreticians of later date analyse the functions of the poet in details, and try to identify the exact part played by Imagination. It is said that Imagination not only presents the totality of experience, -- everfresh beauties, but at the same time presents words and metres, figures and dictions suitable for composition of the desired poetic texture. Rajasekhara emphasizes this aspect of Imagination, and in his endeavour to draw the line of demarcation between imagination belonging to the artist and imagination belonging to the connoisseur says that, while the former supplies expressions and contents, techniques and styles, necessary for construction of poetical paintings, the latter enables the reader to feel his oneness with the artist -- to be one with him. It is repeatedly emphasized that, it is this feeling of oneness which is essential to attainment of poetic experience. Jagannatha of much later date equally emphasizes the role of imagination in construction of poetical paintings, and explains the faculty of imagination as a faculty which presents expressions and contents favourable to creation of the poem, competent to give expression to the complex unified experience and feeling of the poet.

All this shows that Indian Aesthetics conceives of Imagination as a strong faculty competent to integrate the fragmented experiences occurring in the mind of the individual artist and to create a new world of order. That this new world created by the imagination of the poet is different from the world of empirical existence is repeatedly harped at in Indian theory, which states that while the ordinary creation is regulated by the laws of nature, the creation of the literary artist is completely unfettered: it is neither controlled by any external agency nor regulated by any set of rules. This leads us to the doctrine relating to autonomy in Poetry. Indian theory envisages autonomy in the realm of Poetry and states that the literary artist surpasses even the supreme creator in points of authority and autonomy. Anandavardhana states that in the new land of poetry the artist is the supreme creator; the world takes a new shape according to his inclinations and propensities. All this shows that, the art-form has got an independence of its own, and it is surcharged with more profound truth than the real form, implying thereby that, the art is more significant than the real and that perfect autonomy exists in the realm of art.

Section III

Tradition and Novelty

In his attempt to describe the relation which the individual poet is to bear to 'Tradition', T.S. Eliot says that, the poet is required to know the mind of his country, -- the mind of the nation as a matter of fact, before laying his hands upon construction of Poetical Paintings. He further says that, as the mind of the nation flows through the minds of different great poets, whose creations acquire lasting fame, this mind is to be ascertained through acquaintance with a number of poetical creations, emanating from the pens of great artists. Since every poet worth the name respects the 'Tradition', and the mind of the nation is given expression to in different manner by poets of different calibres, in the field of literary art the value of Poetry is to be determined by taking into account the whole gamut of literature. This means that the value of the present specimen of literary art is to be adjudicated by having a look at the past specimens of poetic art, reflecting the mind of the nation in their own ways, and taking a total view of the whole literature.

Continuing his argument that, 'Tradition' is to be given due emphasis in a specimen of Literary Art and that the excellence of the present document is to be considered in the background of the whole gamut of literature, T.S. Eliot maintains that, what holds good of the present, equally holds good of the past. To state more clearly, the value of a specimen of art, which is produced today is determined by the value of the specimens of art that preceded the present specimen, and the values of the past specimens of art are equally altered by the present specimen itself. Eliot is of opinion that the existing order does never complete itself or, so to say, there is no such thing as the "existing order" of work of Art, because with the genesis of new documents of literary art reflecting the mind of the nation in a new way, the existing order is to be altered, making it necessary to re-adjust the values of each work of art towards the whole. This assertion of T.S. Eliot is extremely significant, because it enunciates a new principle of literary evaluation, according to which the excellence of a document of Literary Art is to be adjudicated not merely by analysing the splendour of the poetic tissue or the nature of the feeling residing in the poem, but by the relation which the Poetry under consideration bears to all Poetry including that which originated in the past.

When Eliot says that 'Tradition' or the minds of the poet's COUNTRY is to be comprehended fully by the Artist before laying his hands upon construction of Poetical Paintings, he accepts the greatness of Tradition, and tenders advice to literary artists to bow down to this 'Tradition', because it is the expression of the mind of the nation "that does not superannuate either Shakespeare or Homer". Literary Artists are free to introduce innovations into their techniques and novelty in their plans and plots, but every care is to be taken to see that the mind of the nation is not suppressed under these innovations and novelties. This mean that in the view of T.S. Eliot, there is ample scope for the literary artists to introduce changes and novelties, because without this, the specimen of Art is sure to prove itself boring and bereft of enchantment. While introducing these changes and giving the demonstration of the freshness of his Imagination, the poet is to remain aware of the mind of his own country, which, as Eliot emphasizes, is "much more important than his own private mind".

The relation which the poet's private mind should bear to the mind of his own country, -- the mind of the nation, to which he belongs, -- the relation which individual talent of the poet should bear to 'Tradition' as a whole, is thus extremely complex. The poet is to give expression to his individual talent and the feelings of his private mind, but he is required to remain fully aware of the mind of the country and the nation, and to keep his personal mind subservient to it. A specimen of Poetic Art in which the feeling of the private mind of the poet gains prominence is unable to prove itself enchanting to the connoisseur, because in such a situation the reader feels it difficult to identify himself with the artist and experience the feelings lying confined within the private mind of the poet. A specimen of Poetic Art, on the other hand, in which the private mind of the artist surrenders itself to the mind of the nation, -- the great 'Tradition', emphasised by T.S. Eliot, it becomes possible for the reader to identify himself easily with the artist and the situation, enabling his mind to share the experience of the mind of the nation, flowing through the whole bulk of grand literature. Giving expression to this profound truth in a marvellous way, T.S. Eliot exclaims "what happens is a continual surrender of himself as he is at the moment to something which is more valuable". As the process of creation continues, the literary artist surrenders himself to the 'Tradition', -- makes his own personality subservient to the mind of the nation, and by doing this he acquires greatness, as the grand and the beautiful finds common habitat in the specimen of Literary Art.

While Wordsworth describes Poetry as an expression of poetic personality and defines Poetry as emtoion recollected in tranquility, Eliot floats the new concept of 'Tradition', and describes the poetic process as a process of continual self-secrifice, - a continual extinction of personality.[9] A look at the standpoint of Indian Aesthetics on this issue may at this moment throw new light on the whole problem of creation, because the concept of 'depersonalization' was floated by Indian Aesthetics long back. According to Indian theory, as a matter of fact, in both the processes of literary creation and literary appreciation, personalities are to be rendered docile, because where personality gathers prominence, poetic circuit does not complete itself.

Anandavardhana, the brilliant exponent of the doctrine of 'dhvani', raises this problem of 'depersonalization' in the sphere of creative process, and states that, in his endeavour to remain faithful to the 'Tradition', -- the mind of the nation, it is necessary for the Poet to draw the subject-matter from great poems, emanating from the pens of master artists. In this connexion, Anandavardhana refers to the great epics, the Ramayana and the Mahabharata as the Poems, the emotional appeal of which is fixed and determined from the beginning, and tenders advice to poets of posterity to follow these subject-matters without trying to create any improper innovation in them. It is asserted that such improper innovations are likely to prove detrimental to the main emotional mood, and consequently this is to be avoided. Anandavardhana employs the term 'Siddharasa' to signify such grand poems as the Ramayana and the like, and expresses the opinion that it is always safe for the literary artist to draw the materials of his Poem from such works, since the emotive content is widely known and, consequently, it becomes possible for the connoisseurs to identify themselves with the situations presented in the poem with ease.

In the last chapter of his *Dhvanyaloka*, Anandavardhana raises the question as to whether such drawal of incidents from the epics and grand poems, reflecting the mind of the nation is in a position to make the Poetry stale and disenchanting. In furnishing an answer to this question Anandavardhana says that, the dexterity of the poet in handling the function of suggestion in diverse manner is quite able to impart freshness to the document of Literary Art. This shows that Anandavardhana is quite aware of the necessity of the poet's honouring the 'Tradition', the mind of the country and the nation, but at the same time, he feels that novelty is to be introduced by the literary artist in order to keep the poetry free from the defect of repetition. In his endeavour to strike the balance between surrender to 'Tradition' and induction of freshness, Anandavardhana refers to the principle of 'Rasa', and says that once the imagination of the Literary Artist is able to enshrine 'Rasa' in his document of literary art, the specimen of poetry acquires ever-lasting freshness; such a specimen of poetic art always looks fresh like trees in vernal season.[10]

This means that the great poet is required to enshrine

'Rasa', a dominant emotional mood in his document of Literary Art in such a way that, the main emotional mood becomes able to overpower the total consciousness of the connoisseur and emerge as the main mood in the Poem. This assertion extends an opportunity to Anandavardhana to analyse the dominant emotional mood of the great Epics, the Ramayana and the Mahabharata. The Ramayana, Anandavardhana says, is the external manifestation of the Tragic, and diverse inserted instead throughout the Epic lead to expression of this Tragic. In a similar manner, Anandavardhana continues, all the incidents incorporated in the greatest Epic, the Mahabharata lead to expression of the Quietistic. The question naturally arises as to how the paintings of war and conspiracy, political confabulations and philosophical disquisitions can lead to the revelation of the Quietistic, the basic feeling of which is represented by aversion to the worldly affairs. Anandavardhana gives a long reply to this objection and taking the Mahabharata as a single poetical creation concludes that the Epic has for its dominant mood the Quietistic.[11] The discussion is extremely interesting, but since it has no bearing on the issue it is not being elaborated at the present moment.

Anandavardhana, thus, makes it clear that the literary artist is to honour the mind of the country and the mind of the nation, but, at the same time, he is required to handle with meticulous care the function of Suggestion, so that everlasting freshness can be imparted to the document of Literary Art. It is said with all emphasis that, a plot or a situation, a character or a basic feeling, even though utilised by hundreds and thousands of literary artists does not lose its enchantment like the essential matter of the world, provided the literary artist is endowed with powerful imagination, competent to trigger properly the function of Suggestion into action.

In this connexion, Anandavardhana introduces the concept of "agreement with the mind of the nation", which is technically known as "Samvada" in the terminology of Indian

Aesthetics, and says that, it is very much possible for a poem to respect the mind of the nation and, at the same time, to induct novelty into its own self. This agreement with the mind of the nation appears in three situations: the first, in which the new work appears as a reflection of the old ones, enshrining the mind of the country; the second, in which the new work appears as a painting of the old ones expressing the mind of the nation in its fullness; the third, in which the new poem shines in a poetic texture similar to that of the old poems, but nevertheless, is ensouled by the same mind of the nation. In describing the relative excellence of these three types of "agreement with the mind of the country", Anandavardhana says that, the first two are to be avoided, because they are likely to vitiate the poem with the defect of repetition and consequently to make the new Poem appear as stale and dry. The third type of 'Samvada', on the other hand, is to be admired, because the poetic texture of the new poem in this type is similar to that of the old creation, and at the same time the mind of the nation flows in the same manner through this poem also.[12] It is this flow of the mind of the nation, that does not superannuate Vyasa and Valmiki, and it is this flow that is competent to induct ever-lasting enchantment into new poetic creations. Anandavardhana, thus, introduces the concept of "agreement with Tradition", which he calls 'Samvada' and by pointing out to the relative excellence of the three types of 'agreements' shows how the imaginative faculty of the literary artist is in a position to impart freshness in a document of literary art. Though Anandavardhana praises the dexterity of the literary artist in employment of the function of Suggestion, he favours the idea of respecting 'Tradition' showing thereby that 'Tradition', is of fundamental importance in the creative process, and that the personal feeling of the poet is not that important as the mind of the nation, which is, but another name of 'Tradition'.

It is interesting to note that Tagore emphasizes the concept of the 'mind of the nation', and asserts that both in History and Literature, this mind is to be reflected in its fulness. In his numerous essays on Literature and Literary Criticism, Tagore tries to identify the 'mind of India', and says that only that literature, which has been able to reflect the mind of the nation in its greatness and grandeur has been able to acquire lasting celebrity and eternal enchantment. In his eagerness to locate this mind, Tagore analyses the Vedas and the Upanishads and says that the endeavour of this mind has always been to establish harmony among irreconcilable and to trace unity in diversity. In this connexion, he refers to the grand concept of 'Brahman' or the Supreme Spirit, which is said to reside in all entities and serve as the common bond between diverse aspects of man and nature. Tagore has the feeling that with the discovery of this great synthesising principle of the Supreme Spirit, the search of Indian mind stops; it realises the fulfilment of man's journey and ascertains the fact that, the Supreme Spirit constitutes the goal of all endeavours. Tagore advises the poets of posterity to know this 'mind of Indian nation' and to reflect the craving of this mind to trace unity in diversity in their literary creations, because only by doing this, the literary artists can achieve greatness.[13]

Expanding this principle as enunciated by Tagore and applying it to the practical field of literary creations in the Indian scene, it is possible to say that Poets like Vyasa, Valmiki and Kalidasa, who have been able to reflect the mind of the nation in their literary creations and accept the 'Tradition' have created specimens of sublime Poetry. When this tendency to catch the mind of the nation disappears, the artist's surrender of his self to Tradition takes a good-bye, what is created appears as stale and disenchanting. The literary creations springing in Indian scene after Kalidasa are, therefore, marked by degeneration in taste and artificiality in form. When Indian poetry comes at the crossroads and suffers from lack of inspiration on account of the refusal of the artists to surrender their intellect to the "mind of the nation" and to leave their endeavour to give an exhibition of their dexterity in literary craftsmanship, what is produced is simply 'Pictorial Poetry', bereft of spirit. To rescue literature from this situation, Sankaracharya propounds his new Philosophy in which the common bond of the Supreme Spirit is emphasised again, and an exhortation is made to man to surrender his personal desires to the Absolute. Not only in his philosophical creations, but also in his numerous Devotional Lyrics, Sankaracharya gives expression to this philosophy in regard to the mind of the nation, which casts profound influence on philosophical, literary and sociological speculations of the country. With his philosophical speculations and literary creations Sankara, thus, effects a revival of Tradition and fixes once for all the direction of Literature and Philosophy in India. Sankara, therefore, is not only a great philosopher; his contribution to Indian Literature and Literary Criticism is equally significant.[14]

All this shows that T.S. Eliot emphasises the necessity of 'Tradition', because as he says, it is the 'mind of the nation' that does not superannuate poets. He gives expression to the idea that the poet is required to surrender himself completely to 'Tradition' and 'the mind of the nation' and the process of creation of Poetry is a continuous process of self-denial and 'depersonalization'. Indian Aesthetics shower's profuse praise in equally eloquent terms on 'Tradition' and proclaims that the path shown by great poets is to be followed, because these literary artists know the mind of the nation well. To keep Literary Creations free from the defect of staleness and repetition, Indian Aesthetics speaks further of certain techniques, that are to be adopted by the artists in order to impart freshness to their literary creations. This means that the Imagination of the Poet is to remain sufficiently active at the time of creation of poetry, because it is this faculty which makes it possible for the Poet to utilise the function of Suggestion and induct eternal charm into his poetry. It may appear to be in contradiction to the concept of 'depersonalization', but it will be seen later that the idea of depersonalisation is projected in strongest terms by Indian Aesthetics in diverse contexts; it is acclaimed times without number as the supporting pillar of the superstructure of Aesthetic Realisation.[15]

REFERENCES

1. Tradition and the Individual Talent : T.S. Eliot, para 3, p. 38 (*Selected Prose of T.S. Eliot*, Faber and Faber, London).
2. śaktirnipuṇatā loka-kāvya-śāstrādyavekṣaṇāt / kāvyajñaśikṣayā'bhyāsa iti hetustadudbhave //
—*Kāvyaprakāśa* : Mammata I.3.
3. santi siddharasaprakhyā ye ca rāmāyaṇādayaḥ / kathāśrayā na tairyojyā svcchā rasavirodhinī //
—*Dhavanyāloka* : Ānandavardhana, III (p. 182, Nirnayasagar Edition, Bomay).
4. dṛṣṭapūrvā api hyarthāḥ kāvye rasaparigrahāt / sarve navā ivābhānti madhumāsa iva drumāḥ //
—Ibid., IV, p 293.
5. Sanchayita, Sonar Tari, Puraskar, p. 178.
6. The Metaphysical Poets : T.S. Eliot, p. 64 (*Selected Prose of T.S. Eliot*, Faber and Faber, London).
7. The Hero as Poet : Thomas Carlyle, pp. 244-245 (*English Critical Essays : Nineteenth Century*, Oxford).
8. An Answer to the Qustion What is Poetry : James Henry Leigh Hunt, pp. 256-258 (*English Critical Essays : Nineteenth Century*).
9. Poetry and Poetic Diction : William Wordsworth, pp. 22-23 (*English Critical Essays : Nineteenth Century*).
10. Vācaspatisahasrāṇāṃ sahasrairapi yatnataḥ / nibaddhāpi kṣayaṃ naiti prakṛtirjagatāmiva //
—*Dhvanyāloka* : Ānandavardhana, p. 306.
11. Ibid., pp. 298-300.
12. *Dhvanyāloka* : Ānandavardhana, pp. 306-307.
13. *Prachin Bharater Eka Dharma : Tagore.*
14. *Carpaṭapañjarikā, Gaṅgāstrotra,* etc.: Śaṅkarācārya.
15. vigalitaparimitapramātṛtvabhāvena pramātrā … carvyamāṇo rasaḥ. —*Rasagaṅgādhara* : Jagannātha, Chapter I.

CHAPTER II

Poet the Person and Poet the Artist

Section I

Eliot's views on the Distinction

T.S. Eliot gives a new definition of 'Tradition' and says that the poet is required to bow down to this 'Tradition', which is but another name of the 'mind of the nation'. In describing the process of literary creation, he says that this process is a process of continual self-sacrifice, because the literary artist is required to sacrifice his own personal feelings at the altar of the 'mind of the nation'. It is this analysis of the personality in the process of creation of Poetry that gives a distinct stamp to the critical essays of T.S. Eliot and invests them with deepest truth, which is not traceable in most of the English critical essays.

Eliot feels that the distinction between the maturity of a literary artist and immaturity of another is not to be adjudicated by making an analysis of poetic personality; on the other hand, this evaluation is to be made by making a critical appraisal of the 'finally perfected medium' employed by the two artists. This implies that in the scheme of T.S. Eliot, the Poem is more important than the Poet, and the emotion residing in the Poem is to be taken into account rather than the personal feeling of the Poet. In this connexion Eliot introduces the parallelism of the catalyst, and says when two gases are mixed in the presence of a filament of platinum, they form sulphurious acid. It is further said that, this combination takes place only if the platinum is present; nevertheless, the newly formed acid does not contain any trace of platinum, and the platinum does also remain unaffected, – inert, neutral and unchanged. Expanding this observation, further, Eliot says that, the mind of the poet is the shred of platinum. The presence of this mind, full of certain capabilities and feelings enables the experience of the personál mind to blossom forth into universal experience of the artist, but neither the mind of the man is affected by the universal experience nor is the universal experience itself affected by the feelings of the man who experiences. Thus Eliot clearly draws the line of demarcation between 'the mind that suffers' and experiences, and 'the mind which creates', and asserts that 'the more perfect the artist, the more completely separate in him is the man who suffers and the mind which creates'.

In this connection, Eliot draws the line of distinction between emotions and feelings, and says that the experience which takes a new shape in the presence of the sensitive mind of the poet, is comprised of two element — emotions and feelings. By 'emotion' he refers to those mental states that are of permanent nature and that abide in the form of latent impression in the mind of all men irrespective of caste, creed, religion and country of residence. This emotion again is not 'raw emotion' or 'brute emotion', as the psychologists understand, but 'pure emotion' evolved through a constant sociocultural process. 'Feelings', on the other hand, are just susceptibilities and sympathies, which are incapable of being categorised as love or hatred, tragic or comic, disgustful or quietestic. T.S. Eliot thinks that the experience of a work of art differs in its effect from the experience emanating from a specimen of non-art, because in the experience emanating from a specimen of real art, one comes across a combination of several emotions and various feelings; these emotions and feelings may be complex and of varied nature, but the ultimate experience appears as the totality of all discrete experiences. Individual poet may derive a number of experiences from nature and life, situation and circumstance, but these are ordinary. When the mind of the literary artist is put into action, ordinary experience is transmuted into extraordinary one, and the experience which is generated in the mind of the literary artist is a combination of complex emotions, which live in the poem and not in the individual poet. In describing the mind of the literary artist and the tremendous power possessed by it, Eliot says that the poet's mind is a receptable for catching and storing up numerous feelings and phrases; and images remain there until all the particles are united to form a new compound, and this compound, — the transmuted emotion has its habitat in the poem and not in the individual poet. In this way Eliot proceeds to substantiate the proposition that the poet does not have 'personality' to express, but a particular medium, which is only a medium and not a personality, —a medium, in which impression and experience combine in a peculiar and unexpected way. The way in which Eliot, thus, draws the line of demarcation between the individual poet and the poet— the literary artist - 'the mind of the man who experiences' and 'the mind of the man who creates' is, thus, amazing and quite significant from the point of view of analysis of the process of creation.[1]

It is curious to note that though in the critical essay entitled *Tradition and the Individual Talent*, as also in some other essays T.S. Eliot extol the proposition of 'Impersonality in Art', in his Essay entitled *Yeats,* he describes the poems of W.B. Yeats as the manifestation of strong and unique personality of the artist. This he does in course of drawing the distinction between poems that he calls 'anthology-pieces, and poems of longer duration', which make the readers extremely curious about the mind of the poet operating in diverse areas. The poems, that usually find place in Anthologies give the reader complete satisfaction and delight, and these readers do not feel inclined to have a look at the other compositions of the poet.[2] There are other poems which are, as Eliot says, 'not necessarily so perfect or complete', that they make the readers curious to know more of the poet, because he has a feeling that the poem in question gives only an idea of a fraction of the mind of the literary artist. Poems emanating from W.B. Yeats, Eliot thinks, belong to the second category; they make the readers sit up in excitement and eagerness to learn more about the author's mind and feelings. These poems express the unique personality of the literary artist.

Eliot himself recognises this contradiction between the viewpoints projected in the critical essay entitled '*Yeats*' and the essay entitled '*Tradition and the Individual Talent*' in regard to the doctrine of 'Impersonality in Art'; he raises the issue and gives a solution to it in his endeavour to reconcile the divergent theories. He propounds two forms of 'Impersonality': one which is natural to the more skilful craftsman, implying thereby that, the literary art itself is in a position to give the personal experience an impersonal character, and the second, which is more and more achieved by the mature artist, where the particular emotional experience of the poet is converted into a generalised emotional symbol. In his attempt to expound this classification of Impersonality into two categories, Eliot refers to the lyrics of Lovelace, and Suckling, --poems, which find a place in anthologies and says that, the literary art employed by the poet in these poems is itself in a position to generalise the emotive experience of the artist to some extent. The second type of Impersonality is of higher degree; this appears in the mature poet, who starts from particular emotive experience, but at the same time is capable of expressing a general truth, so much so that, in his poems the particularities of the individual's experience are retained; but at the same time, a general symbol also emerges, making it possible for all readers to share the universalized experience of the artist. Eliot is of opinion that W.B. Yeats gives expression to both types of impersonalities in his poems. Thus he cites the names of the Poems entitled 'A Dream of Death' and 'When you are old and grey and full of sleep' and says that these are beautiful poems no doubt, but the splendour of the literary craftsmanship only gives a universalised form to the particular emotive experience. The poems entitled 'Folly being Comforted' and 'Adam's Curse', on the other hand, give expression to the particularities of the emotional experience of the artist, but the particular experience is converted into a general symbol, as a result of which the poet does not speak for himself alone, but for humanity at large. In this connection, Eliot cites the great lines from

"Pardon that for a barren passion's sake,

All I had come close on fortynine, . . ."

and says that the naming of the age of the poet is significant, inasmuch as, it makes the readers share the universal experience of the man, when he crosses the half span of life time.[3]

In this significant essay '*Yeats*', Eliot analyses the influence exerted by great poets preceding Yeats as also forceful literary movements emerging in Europe during his time, and says that, though Yeats has been able to absorb all these influences, he has been able to approach problems of life with exceptional honesty and courage, as a result of which, it has become possible for the young readers to appreciate the poet more than the old ones. A poet is a man capable of having different experiences in different situations, and with advance in age and change in situation he finds himself in different world in every decade of his life. As this process is a continuous process, and as the poet sees the world with different eyes through advancement in age, the material of his art is continually renewed. It is a tragedy, however, that most of the poets are not in a position to show this adoption to the years. According to T.S. Eliot, W.B. Yeats is one of the very few poets who have been able to demonstrate this 'exceptional honesty and courage' to face the change, as a result of which his poems, particularly the poems of later years are appreciated more by young men. The reason is obvious; the young can see in him the poet operating at his best, because he gives expression to the passion and action of youth with honesty and courage. The old, however, are reluctant to accept the honest statements without fear and shock.

They are shocked by such revelation of what men really is and remains. This means that, as Yeats gives expression to his particular emotional experience with honesty and courage, and at the same time, tries to convert these particularities into general symbols, the young finds it easy to identify him with the artist, and every man for that reason. The old, however, is shocked to find expression of this particular experience: he refuses to accept the proposition that he is like that. In his endeavour to bring this point home, Eliot quotes four lines, which contain bold statements of passions finding their habitat in old age even and says that the lines are impersonal, but not very pleasent, and consequently are not acceptable to the old. These lines are as follows:

"You think it horrible with lust and rage,

Should dance attendance upon my old age

They were not such a plague when I was young:

What else have I to spur me into song?"

These lines are very impressive, but are not pleasant to all, because they represent the personal confessions of a man, who, as Eliot thinks "was essentially the same as most other men; the only difference being in greater clarity, honesty and vigour". Readers, who are shocked to face truth, when expressed with clarity, honesty and vigour may find Eliot's poems disenchanting, but because of the competence of the literary artist to face the real situation of life and experience of the common man with exceptional honesty and courage, clarity and vigour, the real connoisseurs consider the poems as specimen of Sublime Poetry, able to retain its enchantment for all time to come. What Eliot says is that when a particular poet speaks for every man and converts his own particularised emotional experience into general symbols, he becomes able to compose Great and Sublime Poetry, - Poetry that is enchanting for all because in this specimen of poetry he does not speak for himself alone, but for every man. This becomes possible for the poet only when he becomes able to identify himself with every man and all men.

'Impersonality' as projected by Eliot is not contradictory

to the concept of "expression of personality", because a great artist is to start from his intense and personal experience, but at the same time, he is required to express a general truth. Particularities of emotional experience of the literary artist are retained no doubt, but at the same time, they are converted into general symbols, making it possible for all readers to trace their own emotional experience in these symbols. This becomes possible for a literary artist of superior calibre who can identify himself with every man and present his emotional experience in such a way that every man is able to trace his experience in this experience of the artist. This, Eliot affirms, is rendered possible by the imaginative power of the artist: this faculty enables him to identify himself with every man to pick up his emotional experience and give expression to a general experience, retaining at the same time the particularities of his own experience. In case of a great poet, the particularities provide the material for the general truth. This journey of poetry from the land of particularity to the higher region of universality is rendered possible by the strong imaginative power of the literary artist. Thus, Eliot reconciles the concept of 'unique personality of the poet' with the philosophy of 'Impersonality in Art', and says that, when one goes deep into the process of artistic creation, the contradiction vanishes and the conflict disappears. So far as W.B. Yeats is concerned, Eliot exclaims; "the lyric poet and Yeats was always lyric, even when dramatic - can speak for every man, or for men far different from himself; but to do this he must for the moment be able to identify himself with every man or other men; and it is only his imaginative power of becoming this that deceive some readers into thinking that he is speaking for and to himself alone - especially when they prefer not to be implicated."

Section II

Indian Aesthetics on the Issue

Indian Aesthetics recognises this distinction and draws a clear-cut line of demarcation between 'the mind which experiences' and 'the mind which creates'. Anandavardhana, the propounder of the Doctrine of Dhvani regards the symbolic content as the essence of poetic creation and expresses the opinion that, it is the competence of the literary composition to effect revelation of the symbolic that distinguishes a poetic composition from the ordinary linguistic composition. In the view of Anandavardhana, the symbolic appears in three aspects: in the aspect of a fact, in the aspect of a figure and in the aspect of an emotional mood. A case of suggested fact is exemplified by the common Prakrit stanza, which means as follows: "Move about freely, oh! religious-minded friend! that dog has been slain today by the mighty lion that has made the grove situated on the bank of the river Godavari its permanent habitat." In expounding this stanza, Anandavardhana points out that, when one takes note of the speciality of the speaker and the person spoken to, the suggested sense that a covert hint is given to the man not to move about freely is comprehended. The expressed meaning in the verse, thus, is represented by affirmation, while the suggested meaning takes the shape of negation. Anandavardhana says all these to establish his contention that the suggested differs from the expressed in all its aspects.

A case of a suggested figure is exemplified by the verse which means as follows:

"You have filled the horizons of the quarters with the loveliness of your smiling face: as the ocean does not display tremors even on seeing your face in full bloom, it seems that it is a bundle of waters and stupidity." In explaining this stanza, Anandavardhana points out that, the comprehension of the expressed meaning of the verse gives rise to understanding of the implicit idea which is represented by a suppressed Metaphor. The idea is that, the poet wants to present the lovely face of the girl with the character of the moon superimposed on it, because it is at moon-rise alone that the sea displays tremors on its surface and becomes turbulent. This sense of superimposition, however, has not been expressed through a compound or through a direct expression: it has been raised into comprehension through the function of suggestion. The suggested figure, therefore, is definitely distinct from the expressed figure.

So far as the suggestive emotive experience is concerned, Anandavardhana gives the simple reply that, the emotive experience is incapable of being communicated through expression, because the simple naming of a 'Rasa' does not tantamount to its presentation through the medium of poetry. In order to communicate an emotive experience through the medium of poetry, the poet is required to present excitants and accessories, ensuents and moods, sympathies and susceptibilities, and the poetical painting constructed to project these factors with the help of literary craftsmanship raises into comprehension the splendid emotive experience. The aesthetic experience, therefore, is communicated through the function of suggestion alone, and the ordinary function of communication does not help the connoisseur, in any way, in sharing the emotive experience of the literary artist.[4] The excitants and ensuents, characters and situations, permanent moods and transitory feelings, sympathies and susceptibilities, that are required to suggest the emotive experience have been referred to by T.S. Eliot by the expression "Objective Correlative". Since the concept of 'Objective Correlative' is a difficult one and needs elaboration, a separate chapter is being devoted to it later.[5]

In his endeavour to establish the relative excellence of the three categories of the symbolic, Anandavardhana says that, the suggested emotional mood represents the symbolic par excellence, and naturally constitutes the soul of the poetic creation. The considered opinion of Anandavardhana is that, the suggested emotive experience constitutes the real goal of poetry: the suggested fact and the suggested figure terminate ultimately in suggestion of emotive experience, and consequently they are to be regarded as means, and not the goal of the art of poetry. In this connexion, Anandavardhana analyses the tradition in regard to genesis of Poetic Art, the Ramayana represents the external manifestation of the Tragic, generated in the mind of Valmiki on listening to the pitiful lamentations of the she-quail at the slaying of its mate. Abhinavagupta, a brilliant exponent of Anandavardhana utilises this opportunity in expounding the different stages in the process of creative art and says that, while Valmiki, the individual experiences ordinary grief, Valmiki, the literary artist experiences the Tragic, which, undoubtedly, has for its chief ingredient grief and sorrow, but which ultimately takes the shape of unmixed bliss, extending an opportunity to the mind to experience perfect repose. In describing the details of the creative process, Abhinavagupta says that when the artist in his individual capacity listens to the pitiful lamentations of the bird, his mind experiences sorrow; when he starts contemplating on this sorrow, what appears in him is the Tragic, and it is this Tragic that overpowers his mind and as it comes out of his mental plane it takes the shape of the Ramayana, - the first specimen of Poetic Art. Abhinavagupta scrupulously maintains this distinction between the 'mind which experiences', when the artist remains conscious of his individuality and the 'mind which creates', when the artist takes recourse to contemplation and through this process is lifted to a higher state, reaching which he realises his identity with all members of the humanity, so much so that, he becomes in a position to speak not for himself alone, but for all men. In this connection Abhinavagupta introduces the parallelism of water flowing outside a jar when the jar becomes filled up with it completely: he says that, exactly the same process happens in the case of the literary artist as he starts his creative action: the mind of this creative artist becomes full of the Tragic enabling him to realise the greatness of humanity lying latent in him, and it is only after this that the process of creation operates.[6]

A start in regard to this Doctrine is furnished by the great literary critic Bhattanayaka, who affirms that, as long as the mind of the creative artist is not full with sublime emotive experience, poetry is not produced, because he is not able to give expression to his splendid experience. Though

Abhinavagupta draws support in regard to his proposition from the statement of Bhattanayaka cited above, he proceeds to reject another contention of the same literary critic, the contention relating to the distinction between the Sastra and the Kavya. Bhattanayaka expresses the opinion that, while in the Sastra, the expression is of paramount importance, and in the historical work it is the import that is of real significance, in the Kavya both the expression and the content are subordinated to the process of communication. Abhinavagupta is prepared to accept this contention of Bhattanayaka, if by process of 'communication' he refers to the function of suggestion, because it is the function of suggestion that really constitutes the salient trait of Poetry.

While Bhattanayaka expends his energy in drawing the line of distinction between the Sastra and the Kavya, Rajasekhara tries to effect linkage between the two, while indicating their difference, implying thereby that divine inspiration plays a prominent role in creation of poetic art. Rajasekhara mentions two categories of composition: the Sastra and the Kavya. He says that the knowledge of the scripture, i.e., diverse branches of learning is necessary for composition of a specimen of poetic art. Rajasekhara initiates a discussion on the Sastra first of all. He classifies scientific knowledge concerning the branches of learning, technically referred to as the sastra into two categories: that which is a gift from above and is incapable of being accepted as emanating from the passion and action of a human agency, and that which is capable of being accepted as an article or work composed by a human being. To the first category belongs the entire Vedic literature, which has been handed down by 'Tradition' from ancestors to the posterity and in regard to which only the names of seers are applicable. Tradition mentions the names of different sages to whom the Vedas are supposed to have been revealed, as a result of which the entire Vedic literature is regarded as a revealed composition and the seers are regarded as experts engaged in contemplation, men to whom certain verified and verifiable truths had been revealed in the morning of mankind. Indian Tradition, thus, regards the sages as seers, – the first persons to catch the laws of nature, which had been operating since creation of the universe. These laws of nature are eternal, and consequently, with reference to them it is not possible to conceive of a composer or a creator: at best one can think of a discoverer, – a man, who can locate the law, – the eternal truth for the first time. This exactly happens in case of the eternal truths, projected in the Vedic literature.[7]

So far as the second category of speech represented by the Kavya or Poetry is concerned, Rajasekhara mentions that poetry also presents certain truths, but these truths flash before the inward eye of the literary artist only when he makes himself acquainted with the truths presented in all the branches of learning, including the Sciences. This linkage which Rajasekhara wants to establish between the Sastra, the main bulk of which represents the 'revealed body' of literature and the Kavya is of profound importance from the point of view of literary criticism, because it shows that to arrive at poetry it is necessary to have acquaintance with diverse branches of learning, because the poetic truth flashes before the inward eye of only that man, whose intellect has been sharpened through acquaintance with diverse branches of Science.

This role played by intellect in genesis of Poetry extends an opportunity to Rajasekhara to leave a discussion on the equipments necessary for the literary artist and also to draw a line of demarcation between the different faculties of the poetic mind, that operate at the material moment of genesis of Poetry. Rajasekhara envisages three categories of Intelligence or Power of Understanding: Recollection, technically known as 'Smriti', which leads to knowledge of the past; Intellect, technically known as 'Mati', which effects understanding of the present, and Vision, technically known as 'Prajna', which effects comprehension of the future. Rajasekhara thinks that, all these three categories of the Power of Understanding are necessary for the poet, because the poet is required to see the past, the present and the future simultaneously, so that the universe can be collected together and reflected in the small compass of a poetical painting. Rajasekhara, thus, emphasizes the 'seeing eye' of the poet, — the 'eye' that enables him to have the total view of the passions and actions of human life as also of the land of nature.[8]

In his endeavour to locate the causal factor of Poetic Creation, Rajasekhara arrives at the proposition that 'contemplation' and constant practice are necessary for genesis of Poetic Art. He refers to the view-points of his predecessor, Shyamadeva, who thinks that the prime factor necessary for creation of poetry is represented by deep contemplation of the literary artist: it is said that, only a mind engaged in deep contemplation can see the past, the present and the future collected together and the poetic truth in its total splendour. Another predecessor of Rajasekhara, Mangala, however, maintains that, constant practice is an essential factor, necessary for creation of poetry, because as he says, practice enables a poet to select appropriate things for his poetical creation and employ literary craftsmanship in an appropriate manner so that, the emotive experience can be transferred from him to the connoisseur. Rajasekhara effects a synthesis between these two views, and declares that contemplation, which is an internal effort and constant practice, which is an external action, both are necessary for genesis of that creative faculty, which constitutes the chief equipment of the literary artist. This means that, Rajasekhara draws a line of demarcation between the different stages in the process of creation of poetry, and says that when contemplation and practice combine, the Poetic Faculty appears, enabling literary artists to locate new truths and construct appropriate poetical paintings. All this shows that Rajasekhara is aware of the distinction between 'the mind which experiences' and 'the mind which creates'. Possibly, he is the only literary critic to identify the process of contemplation as responsible for transformation of the 'experiencing mind' into the 'creating mind'. The poet in his individual capacity gathers experience: thereafter, he starts contemplating on the experience gathered; it is only after this that the Poetic Faculty, necessary for construction of poetical images dawns in him; and he goes on creating specimen of poetic art. The 'mind which experiences', as projected by Eliot corresponds to the mind of the literary artist, before contemplation, as proposed by Rajasekhara; the 'mind which creates', as envisaged by Eliot similarly corresponds to the mind of the poet after contemplation, as suggested by Rajasekhara.

It is equally interesting that Rajasekhara draws a distinction between Poetic Faculty and Poetic Genius. He employs the term 'Sakti' to signify Poetic Faculty, that serves as the germ of poetic creation and applies the expression 'Pratibha' to signify genius, which along with culture is supposed to infuse excellence in Poetic Faculty, making it one of the highest degree.

Rajasekhara conceives of poetic genius or 'Pratibha' as a faculty that presents expressions, contents, poetic figures, literary techniques and other components of literary craftsmanship to the literary artist making it possible for him to see the unseen things and ideas clearly and carve out appropriate paintings, necessary for their objective presentation. He envisages two categories of genius; the genius necessary for the poet and the faculty necessary for the connoisseur, implying thereby that, for appreciation of poetry also, a special faculty is necessary and that the ordinary power of understanding is not in a position to deliver the goods in this case. In regard to the creative genius of the literary artist, it is said that, the deeper the contemplation of the mind which experiences, the more powerful is the poetic faculty serving as the germ of poetic creation. When this is coupled with constant practice and thorough acquaintance with diverse branches of learning, what appears is genius of the highest type, as a result of which it becomes possible for the artist possessed of this Genius to create specimens of great poetry. Rajasekhara says, there are poets and poets, and the difference in appeal pertaining to their compositions is quite palpable; while the poetry of one poet resides in his laboratory alone, the poem of other reaches, the laboratory of friends; the poem of yet another gets itself enshrined in the hearts of connoisseur and travels throughout the universe, enchanting the minds of lovers of poetry.[9]

Rajasekhara asserts that creative faculty is superior to culture, because it is in position to cover up the difficulty and deficiency of the literary artists, springing from lack of culture. In support of this view, he cites the observation of Anandavardhana, who affirms that deficiency springing from lack of culture is capable of being rectified by strong creative genius, but deficiency springing from weakness of creative faculty is incapable of being rectified, inasmuch as, it makes itself felt to every reader, creating thereby a definite disenchantment for the poetry.

Rajasekhara recognises large variety of literary artists and makes gradation among poets according to the strength of creative genius and superiority of culture, springing from acquaintance with creation of master artists and scientific subjects. The best type of the poet is known as the 'Kaviraja', who is supreme in the matter of transmuting his personal feeling into an emotive experience and is capable, at the same time, of creating appropriate poetic symbol, that can surely be translated back into corresponding emotive experience in the mind of the reader. The 'Kaviraja' is supreme in his own field: his poetry is marked by autonomy, and is incapable of being adjudicated through application of ordinary rules of nature, because the laws do not operate in the higher plane. When Rajasekhara describes the higher type of literary art as one supreme in the matter of attainment of emotive experience, as also in the matter of communicating this experience into the mind of the connoisseur, he certainly takes note of the process of transmutation and depersonalization, because unless the component of individuality is dropped, emotive experience cannot be communicated to the connoisseur, as a result of which cannot 'Rasa' manifest itself in it full splendour.

The literary composition of the 'Kaviraja', however, not only shines in the splendour of 'Rasa': it shines also in the grandeur of poetic texture, inasmuch as, it is marked by maturity. In order to signify this concept of maturity, Rajasekhara employs the term 'paka' and says that while the composition of the great literary artists is marked by harmonious blending of language and thought and lustre of the poetic tissue, the writing of the artist of lesser calibre looks pedestrian, being devoid of charmingness of the element of form.

In his endeavour to describe Appreciative Genius, Rajasekhara indicates that appreciative genius belongs to the connoisseur: it is that faculty, which enables the reader to establish his identity with the greatest artist and humanity at large. Due to the functioning of this faculty, it is said, the connoisseur shares the emotional experience of the literary artist and consequently, savours the delight associated with his own self. Appreciative Genius, thus, makes the efforts of the literary artist successful, as otherwise, the poetic circuit would have remained incomplete. This observation of Rajasekhara reminds one of the propositions mooted by Anandavardhana that, knowledge of Grammar and Lexicon does not help in any way the reader in entering into the mystery of poetry: the secret of poetry is located only with the help of a strong critical faculty, which is competent to translate back the literary and art symbol into a corresponding emotive experience in the mind of the connoisseur. It is not without reason, therefore, that Abhinavagupta describes the literary artist and the appreciative reader as the two fractions of the single whole, because the experience of each depends on the experience of the other for completion of the grand circuit.

Rajasekhara himself raises the question as to whether the literary artist also is endowed with appreciative genius, and introduces a detailed discussion on this issue. While some of the theoreticians maintain that the literary artist is endowed with appreciative genius also, Rajasekhara maintains that, the appreciative genius is distinct from the creative genius, and though some literary artists may be endowed with appreciative genius, and some critical connoisseurs with creative genius, the two are distinct from each other; and the existence of one does not necessarily entail the existence of the other. In support of his doctrine, Rajasekhara cites a verse in which the parallelism of the touchstone is introduced and it is said that, just as one slab of stone gives birth to gold, while a different slab tests its genuine character, similarly one endowed with creative genius constructs poetic paintings, while the other possessed of critical faculty evaluates it.

While discussing the relative strength and excellence of creative faculty and culture, which are supposed to lead conjointly to genesis of Poetry, Rajasekhara says that writings of great artists are marked by 'Paka': this, however, is conspicuous by its absence in the writings of poets of lesser calibre. So far as the definition of 'Paka' is concerned, Rajasekhara says that, it consists in establishment of perfect balance between the different expressions employed to construct the poetical painting. When the creative process goes on in the mind of the poet and he continues his search after suitable expressions, his creative genius presents certain forms. Of these the most appropriate one is picked up by his imagination, as a result of which the painting acquires special charm of its own. Maturity in poetic texture, thus, is inducted through establishment of perfect balance between the expressions, so much so that, a single expression becomes incapable of being separated from the whole texture of Poetry. By introducing the concept of 'Paka', Rajasekhara, thus, takes the critical world to the doorway of the Gestalt Theory of Poetry, according to which, a specimen of literary art is incapable of being fragmented into parts. Kuntaka of later date develops this theory; he expounds the concept of 'Vakrata', extolling the balance not only between different expressions, but between different meanings, and between expressions and meanings, as well.[10]

Section III

Tagore on Distinction

In order to have an idea of the process of 'depersonalization' in all its aspects as also to understand the different stages involved in the process of creation of Poetry, it is necessary to enter into the philosophy of Tagore on the process of genesis of Art. In his numerous Essays on Beauty and Aesthetic Experience, Tagore has tried to analyse the concept of 'Beauty' in detail and to find out the linkage between Beauty and Restraint, Beauty and Good, Beauty and Harmony, as also between Beauty and Truth. In most of these Essays, Tagore has given expression to the view that 'Beauty' is closely linked with the concept of 'Restraint', and when these two are combined, what is produced is Good, constituting part and parcel of the highest Truth. He says that, 'Restraint' develops a faculty for appreciation of 'Beauty', and Aesthetic Instinct, in its turn, also attracts the mind towards 'Restraint'. The quality of chastity in a lady implants beauty in her, because, infatuation and emergence of sex-impulses and passions are absent in her case. It becomes possible for the real taster of food to experience the taste of delicious dishes: this is incapable of being enjoyed by the glutton, who does not know restraint and whose attention is fixed more on quality and quantity of dishes served than on the nature of the experience derived. This relation between 'Beauty' and 'Restraint', on the one hand, and 'Beauty' and 'Goodness', on the other, are to be borne in mind before entering into Tagore's Philosophy of Beauty, and the thought structured by him on the distinction between 'Individuality' and 'Personality'.

Tagore gives expression to the view that 'Individuality' manifests itself in the man as long as he remains occupied with the thoughts concerning the necessities of life, – the small fragments of necessary enjoyables and unnecessary involvements, leading to pleasure and pain, hope and despondency. Individuality, thus, is linked with considerations of the truncated ego, – its petty thoughts of gain and loss, necessities and redundancies. 'Personality', on the other hand, is a quality of much higher level: this quality manifests in the man when he forgets his sense of truncated ego and has the realisation that, he is the resort of ever-shining glory of humanity, capable of creating wonders. When the small man has this realisation that, he is a grand member of the great association of Humanity, and has close linkage with the bigger universe, his mind savours the delight of liberation. 'Personality' manifests itself in such a man, and he becomes able to carve out all specimens of Art, including Poetical Painting, competent to reflect the complete universe in its small compass. 'Individuality', thus, manifests itself in the man limited by considerations in regard to exigencies of the ordinary world; 'Personality' manifests itself in the bigger man, able to experience his linkage with the bigger community. Tagore, therefore, describes 'Personality' as 'Creative Personality', and gives expression to the Theory that, the contemplating creative mind which stays in the heart of the hearts of the unfettered and expanded man is the real creator of Art, – the supreme creator competent to give form to inexplicable beauty.

After establishing the linkage which 'Restraint' bears to 'Beauty' Tagore proceeds to establish relations between 'Beauty' and eternal 'Good' as well. In the eyes of Tagore, the distinction between the 'Pleasant' and the 'Good' vanishes altogether, and he maintains times without number that the 'Good' is always 'Beautiful', and that which is 'Beautiful' necessarily leads to supreme 'Good'. This attitude of Tagore is evident in his criticism of the classics of Kalidasa, namely, the Kumarasambhava, the Sakuntala and the Meghaduta. While Kumarasam bhava and Sakuntala present the downfall suffered by love due to absence of restraint, and the reconquest of the Heaven by love when it clothes itself with restraint, the Meghaduta describes the journey of Art as a whole from the land of natural beauty to the land of instinctive beauty, when 'Beauty' finds itself eternally united with Truth and Good. This analysis of Tagore reminds the connoisseur of the famous statement of Keats, – the statement that,

'Beauty is Truth and Truth Beauty'. As a matter of fact, Tagore quotes this observation of Keats many times in his numerous Essays on 'Beauty', and tries to substantiate the statement by citing references from the Upanishads, – the great gospel written in the morning of mankind.

The Upanishads declare that 'Bliss' resides in 'Truth' and 'Beauty'. It says that anything which gets expression is but a form of eternal bliss, – the Absolute, that forms the root of the creation. From dust under feet to the blue horizon and the stars shining high up in the firmament everything represents Truth and Beauty, – the beautiful form of the immortal Absolute. Tagore realises that, the understanding that Truth is steeped in eternal Beauty and Beauty in Truth provides splendid inspiration to man for all time to come; it shows that beyond thoughts concerning the small necessities of life there is a higher level of consciousness, where 'Truth' and 'Beauty' remain unseparable. This, virtually, is a re-statement of the Philosophy of the Upanishads, – the philosophy that the universe springs from 'Bliss', is sustained by 'Bliss' and finally resolves itself into 'Bliss'.[11]

In one of his letters, Tagore draws the attention of readers to a particular saying of the Upanishads, which states that two birds sit in the same branch; of these two, one tastes the fruit and other simply sees. The bird, which simply sees, experiences profound joy, – joy which is sane, pure and unbounded. In explaining this statement, Tagore says that, these two birds live in the same man; one is guided by considerations in regard to exigencies of the ordinary world; the other is not guided by these considerations; it has no necessity to fulfil. The bird, which tastes the fruit carves out a creation, which is bounded by considerations of necessity and purpose; the bird, that simply sees and experiences sane and wholesome pleasure carves out a creation that is unrestricted and unlimited : through this splendid creation it manifests its own bigger self. The bird that tastes the fruit experiences external objects and material that are foreign to its being. The bird that sees experiences its own self, which transcends the limits imposed by the small ego. Tagore affirms that Poetry consists in the splendid Art of giving expression to the expanded self, that transcends the limits imposed by small ego.[12]

The two expressions employed by Indian Theory to refer to the creation of these two selves are extremely significant: the creation carved out by the small ego is usually referred to by the expression 'Nirmana' or 'Nirmiti', which implies that this creation is made to order for the purpose of fulfilling certain purpose: the expression 'Sristi', on the other hand, is employed to signify the sense of the creation carved out by the expanded ego: this creation is not made to order, inasmuch as, the expanded ego creates it in its endeavour to express the abundance of its own self, – 'Bliss' associated with its own being. It is not without reason, therefore, that T.S. Eliot in his preface to the *Sacred Wood* refers to the Art of Poetry as a 'superior amusement', and in explaining it, says that, the Art of poetry is not an amusement for superior people, but rather an amusement of superior type in which the self savours the delight associated with its own being.

The distinction which Tagore draws between 'Individuality', on the one hand, and 'Personality', on the other, is expounded in details in his Essays contained in the collection entitled 'Personality'. In these critical essays Tagore gives expression to the following truths:

(a) In the realm of Art the expanded ego gives expression to its own self. The man who experiences the grandeur of his expanded ego is 'Personal'. As long as the man remains conscious of his necessities of life and mundane possessions, the man which inhabits in him is 'Individual'. This 'Individual' man tries to establish relations with the universe through his own small joys and sorrows, trifling attachments and detachments. The 'Personal' man, on the other hand, establishes relations with the universe without any considerations in regard to personal gain or loss, small hope and despair, petty attachment and non-attachment. Every specimen of Art expresses the 'Personal Man' and not the 'Individual Man':

(b) It is the 'Personality' of the artist that removes the distinction between mind and matter, stream of thoughts and chain of events, and gives rise to the unfragmented total one; it constitues the balancing factor, which cuts at the root of conflict between opposite forces and maintains harmony, as a result of which, the whole one is produced and gets itself expressed in the form of Art

(c) When a chain of events or for the matter of fact, a subject-matter is viewed in its totality with human approach by this 'Personality' lying latent in man, it becomes the subject-matter of Art :

(d) As literature gives expression to this 'Personality' lying latent in man, it necessarily employs the language of picture and music:

(e) In the realm of Poetry, the goal is represented by attainment, and generation of profound 'Bliss':

'Beauty' constitutes the means through which the goal is achieved. This 'Bliss' which is derived from the experience of Poetry is necessarily disinterested.

All this makes it clear that Tagore is extremely conscious of the distinction between 'Individuality' and 'Personality' of the same man. It is because of this that, while presenting anecdotes connected with the lives of Valmiki and Kalidasa, he says that, the materials which are available from the biography of a Poet do not necessarily bear any link with his creations. The biography of a Poet, he says, gives expression to the artist's 'Individuality': his poetical creations, on the other hand, extend an opportunity to the readers to know his 'Personality'. The statement that, the 'Poet is not traceable in his Biography', therefore, is surcharged with profound Truth. In one of the critical essays contained in the collection entitled 'Atmaparichaya', Tagore says that, when he takes retrospective view of his poetical creations, he feels that he had no control over the quality and quantity of his creative art: when he thought that he was writing some poems or creating some specimens of poetical paintings, he could experience that, the writer or artist was someone other that the 'Individual Man'. This 'Personality', as conceived of by Tagore, is the expanded ego, which is not guided by any considerations of necessity and mundane possessions: it does not have any responsibility to discharge or obligation to anybody to fulfil. [13]

It may not be out of place to mention here that, the concept of 'Personality' as projected by Tagore bears close affinities to the thoughts of Croche on 'Personality' and its relations to 'Individuality'. Like Tagore Croche also believes that 'Individuality' is the truncated autonomy of the small ego, which operates within the four walls of mundane possessions and thoughts : this autonomy is a degenerated form of autonomy. By the side of this truncated 'Individuality', there flows a perennial stream of unbounded 'Personality', which enables the artist to realise his identity with the great humanity and through that with the Grand and the Sublime. This pure stream of expanded ego represents the 'Personality' of man : this 'Personality' is the real artist, competent to carve out all specimens of Art. As Croche proclaims: "Thus it is without doubt that if pure Intuition (and pure expression, which is the same thing) are indispensible in the work of Art, the personality of the artist is equally indispensible". [14] This personality, as conceived of by Croche also stay above the level of mundane possessions and dispossessions, earthly joys and sorrows; consequently, it is not tinged by any quality or attribute. This ego of the creative artist is pure and free : it is unattached by any attribute and does not have any obligation to anybody. When in his critical essay, entitled 'Sahityer Tatparya', Tagore says, 'literature does not constitute the creation of an individual man : it represents divine proclamation, because great specimens of Art are always impersonal and universal', he refers to the same truth. This suppression of 'Impersonality' by the element of 'Personality' in Art has been referred to by Keats through the expression 'Negative Capability', employed in one of his letters written to Wood House. The 'Negative Capability' is the capability of the poet to put into slumber his 'Individuality', guided by considerations of mundane possessions and dispossessions: with this suppression of narrow 'Individuality' emerges and shines in its full splendour the expanded ego, through which it can establish its relations with the universe at large. When the fine distinction drawn by Tagore between the concepts of 'Individuality' and 'Personality' is taken into account, the position of T.S. Eliot becomes all the more clear. When Eliot affirms that 'the mind which creates' is different from the 'mind that suffers', he refers definitely to the same process. The 'man who suffers', as conceived by Eliot is the individual man, experiencing small joys and sorrows : the 'mind which creates' is the personality of the artist, which is but another name of humanity at large. When Eliot, therefore, speaks of 'extinction of personality' he refers to extinction of individuality or, in other words, to extinction of the small ego of the creative artist, because, the personality of the artist is indispensible for creation of poetry. As Eliot does not dilate upon the fine distinction between 'Impersonality' and 'Individuality', his writings have created some confusion, but this does not mean, that, he envisages extinction of great personality. 'Impersonality', as conceived of by Eliot, is really 'deindividuality', as projected by Tagore and 'Negative Capability' as introduced by Keats. All these critics thus refer practically to the same condition necessary for genesis of Poetic Art : only they employ different expressions to project their findings.

REFERENCES

1. Tradition and the Individual Talent : T.S. Eliot, pp. 41 (*Selected Prose of T.S. Eliot*, Faber and Faber, London).
2. Yeats : T.S. Eliot, pp. 250 (*Selected Prose of T.S. Eliot*, Faber and Faber, London).
3. Ibid., pp. 251.
4. pratīyamānaṃ punaranyadeva
   vastvasti vāṇīṣu mahākavīnām /
   yat tat prasiddhāvayavātiriktaṃ
   vibhāti lāvaṇyamivāṅganāsu //

   — *Dhvanyāloka* : Ānandavardhana, p. 16.

5. Hamlet : T.S. Eliot, p. 48 (*Selected Prose of T.S. Eliot*, Faber and Faber, London).
6. kāvyasyātmā sa evārthas tathā cādikaveḥ purā /
   krauñcadvandvaviyogotthaḥ śokaḥ ślokatvamāgataḥ //
   — *Dhvanyāloka* : Ānandavardhana with Locana, p. 31.
7. *Kāvyamīmāṃsā* : Rājaśekhara, Chapter II (Oriental Institute, Baroda).
8. Ibid., Chapter IV.
9. ekasya tiṣṭhati kavergṛha eva kāvya-
   manyasya gacchati suhṛdbhavanāni yāvat /
   nyasyadvidagdhavadaneṣu padāni śaśvat
   kasyāpi sañcarati viśvakutūhalīva //
   —Ibid., Chapter IV, p. 13. (same as above).
10. Ibid., Chapter V.
11. Essays contained in the collections '*Sāhitya*' and '*Sāhityer Pathe*' : Tagore (Visva Bharati).
12. Letter dated 20th Baisakh, 1323 Bengali Era : Tagore, *Japan-yatri* (Visva-Bharati).
13. Ātmaparicaya : Tagore.
14. "We donot ask of an artist instructions as to real facts and thoughts nor that he should astonish us with the richness of his imagination, but that he should have a prsonality, in contact with which sentiment of the spectator or hearer may be heated. ... Thus it is without doubt that if pure intuition (and pure expression, which is the same thing) are indispensable in the work of art, the personality of the artist is equally indispensable."

    — *Aesthetic* : Croche.

CHAPTER III

The Means of Communication

Section I

Views of T.S. Eliot

Eliot emphasizes the process of communication of experience in Poetry, and in a number of Critical Essays discusses his position that, the Art of Poetry consists in the process of communication of experience, which at the outset is transformed into general experience, as a result of which it becomes possible for the reader to participate in the splendid universal experience. Eliot considers the 'Meaning' of a poem as insignificant, because it is not the purpose of the literary artist to communicate the stuff of experience, but the experience itself.

While presenting his thoughts on the so-called 'obscurity' of modern poetry, T.S. Eliot raises the question of the role played by meaning in a poem, and expresses the opinion that to a great extent the 'meaning' belongs to prose rather than to poetry, implying thereby that the 'meaning' plays a secondary role in a specimen of Poetic Art. In his Critical Essay entitled *The Use of Poetry and the Use of Criticism*, Eliot says that, the chief use of the 'meaning' of a poem may be to satisfy one habit of the reader, to keep his mind diverted and quiet, while the poem does its work upon him. He goes on to compare the 'meaning' presented by literary artist to a hit of nice meat provided to the house dog by the imaginary burglar, who seizes upon this opportunity of committing burglary quietly. Eliot expresses the view that, it is not the 'meaning' of a poem, that inducts enchantment to it, because the 'meaning', can be ascertained from other sources also. The 'meaning' therefore, seems 'superfluous' to him; it is the means of communication which is of prime importance in poetry, because the literary artist is required to construct a pattern that can symbolise his experience. When the reader gets himself acquainted with this experience, the symbol is translated back into a corresponding experience in his mind.[1]

As the process of communication is the most important factor in poetry, Eliot tries to locate the means, that are necessary for effecting communication of this experience. In his endeavour to search after the factors that are necessary to effect this communication, Eliot arrives at the concept of 'Objective Correlative', a new concept introduced by him. In poetry, 'meaning' is not important: what is important is 'emotion'. And Eliot feels that, the only way of expressing emotion in the form of Art is by finding 'Objective Correlative'. In his attempt to describe the 'Objective Correlative'. Eliot says that, it may be a set of objects, a situation, a chain of events, which may emerge as the formula of that particular emotion: 'such that, when the external facts, which must terminate in sensory experiences are given, the emotion is immediately evoked'. Continuing his elaboration of the concept, Eliot refers to Shakespeares most successful tragedies where, it is asserted, this exact equivalence of emotion is available. Thus, the state of mind of Lady Macbeth walking in her sleep has been communicated by the dramatist through successful accumulation of imagined sensory experience : the words of Macbeth on hearing of his wife's death strike the reader because the sequence of events, followed by these words immediately evoke corresponding emotion in the minds of the connoisseurs. These tragedies are successful, because, as Eliot thinks, the sequence of events, the situations, the set of objects and the expressions are adequate for evocation of emotion: they are neither too heavy nor too light. With reference to these, it cannot be asserted that, a substantial portion can be deleted or a new portion added, because they are inevitable, and at the same time, they are sufficient to evoke the emotion intended to be expressed in the form of Art by Shakespeare.

While *Macbeth* happens to be a successful tragedy of Shakespeare, *Hamlet* is not at all, because the 'Objective Correlative' introduced by the dramatist in this drama is not in a position to evoke the emotion intended to be expressed in the form of Art. This artistic inevitability, Eliot maintains, lies in the complete adequacy of the external set of objects and chain of events to the emotion : and this is what is precisely deficient in *Hamlet.* As Eliot says, Hamlet, the man is dominated by emotion, which is inexpressible, because 'it is in excess of the facts as they appear'. Eliot thus considers emotion as the centre of gravity of Poetic Art; he thinks that the business of the literary artist is to communicate an experience, to evoke an emotion by finding an 'Objective Correlative', by creating a pattern combining situations and characters, chain of events and set of objects, so that, the pattern can evoke a corresponding emotion and experience in the mind of the reader. Of course, according to Eliot, the reader is required to go through a process of 'brain work' in order to enable him to participate in this splendid experience communicated by the poet. Though Eliot introduces the concept of 'Objective Correlative' in his critical essay entitled *Hamlet*, he does not expound this concept in detail in any of his critical essays. In giving a short description of this concept, he simply says that, it may be either a situation or a set of objects or, for that matter, a chain of events. If the literary artist can locate these external factors that are inevitable to evocation of emotion he can be sure of transplanting the desired emotion or an emotion correlated with the desired one in the mind of the connoisseur. The problem of locating this 'Objective Correlative', of creating a pattern by combining characters and situations, chain of events and set of objects, thus, becomes the problem of poetic creation itself. The search after 'Objective Correlative' therefore, is really a search after Poetic Creation itself.[2]

Since the concept of 'Objective Correlative' is a new one, it is necessary to view it from different angles and to arrive at the real intention of Eliot in regard to this concept by analysing his views available in different critical essays. The dictionary meaning of the term 'objective' is a thing or idea not belonging to the consciousness of the perceiving or thinking subject, but, what is presented to this subject, i.e., what is external to the mind; it also refers to the concept of dealing with outward things exhibiting actual facts uncoloured by the exhibitor's feelings and opinion. When these two meanings of the expression 'objective' are taken into account, it becomes evident that Eliot's 'objective' is an external equivalent to emotion. When this meaning is combined with the meaning presented by the expression of 'correlative', it naturally comes to this that the 'Objective Correlative' of Eliot is a verbal equivalent of thought and emotion, an equivalent which is in a position to evoke the desired emotion or an emotion similar to the desired one in the mind of the connoisseur. The experience of the poet is to be transformed into the state of mind by objectifying the emotion. It is, therefore, the duty of the literary artist, Eliot affirms, to objectify the emotion by locating inevitable characters and situations, chain of events and set of objects and by creating an inevitable pattern by combining them.

The 'Objective Correlative', thus, in an object which resides outside the consciousness of the perceiver; nevertheless, it bears a relation to the emotion lying latent in his mind. This existence of contradiction in the very nature of the 'Objective Correlative' gives a new status to it, and shows that the ordinary norms of adjudicating status are not applicable in the realm of Art. The design of effecting a pattern through combination of objective correlatives makes the refined reader detached and at the same time correlated to an emotion. The attachment is from personal streams of thoughts concerning the small ego, and 'relation' is with the latent emotion, an emotion which is shared by humanity at large.

An attempt is also capable of being made to trace the relation between mind and matter in the concept of 'Objective Correlative', because a direct sensuous apprehension of thought is intended to be presented through objective presentation in the 'Objective Correlative'. The concept of 'Objective Correlative', as floated by Eliot, therefore, is a new concept, which effects the linkage between the emotive experience of the literary artist and that of the refined reader. The 'Objective Correlative', at the same time, is a bundle of opposites, inasmuch as, it maintains link between mind and matter, - attachment and detachment.

According to T.S. Eliot, the business of a poet is to communicate his experiences to other men, - to refined readers, possessed of aesthetic sensibility, who have done sufficient 'brain work' necessary to catch the symbol employed by the artist. The feelings, that are aroused in the poet by his experience are common to all normal man. They are connected with normal moral sentiments and raw-emotions and with the factors that excite these. When 'Objective Correlatives' are located by the poet and a pattern created through their employment, similar feelings are aroused in the mind of the connoisseur, as a result of which, the experience of the artist is usually transplanted in him. Eliot believes that a 'fundamental brain work' is an essentiality for the connoisseur; unless this is done, the reader is unable to catch the meaning of the symbols and consequently to translate them back into corresponding experiences in his mind. In his book entitled 'Inter-War English poetry' Prof. M.K. Sen has cited certain 'Objective Correlatives' from the poems of T.S. Eliot and has shown how the emotions have been objectified by symbols. Prof. Sen says, "degenerated indoor life of the times is typified by 'dingy shades in a thousands furnished rooms', by 'smell of steaks in passage ways', and by 'the rattling of breakfast plates in basement kitchen'. These glimpses of modern urban life chiefly typify a phase of civilization. The image of children climbing an apple tree in an orchard and the image of a girl holding in her arms flowers in rain have become symbols of innocent bliss and of frustration respectively". When the reader gets himelf acquainted with the symbols of these experiences, - symbols, that are of wider dimension, competent to work upon the consciousness of as many readers as possible, the particular phase of civilization or the image of innocent bliss, as the case may be, appears in his mental plane, as a result of which he experiences an emotive experience similar to that of the poet. The 'Objective Correlative', thus, serves the purpose that is served by the symbol introduced in the realm of Art by the french symbolist.[3]

Stephen Mallarme, the father of French Symbolism expounds the Doctrine that, in Art suggestive power is to be employed to evoke feelings and emotions in the minds of the connoisseurs, because suggestion has the power of imparting loveliness to the most deformed even. Mallarme rejects the actual and palpable wood of trees and wants the evocation of the feeling of satisfaction and joy through description of shuddering of the trees and silent murmuring of the leaves, – he thinks that to produce a better effect it is necessary to project the symbols, because description of the wood as the cluster of trees is not in a position to impart loveliness to the forests. "To name an object", Mallarme says, "is to destroy enjoyment: to present an idea in an enchanting manner the best way is to suggest it". Mallarme believes in the suggestive power of poetry and declares that higher realities can be expressed only through the medium of musical verse. Being influenced by French Symbolist Movement, Eliot also acknowledges the suggestive power of poetry, and accepts the view that emotions are to be evoked by 'Objective Correlatives', that are to be skillfully employed in the pattern created by the artist. T.S. Eliot also acknowledges the power of music in Poetry, because, as he says, music itself is in a position to cause apprehension of certain feelings, lying latent in the man. The difference between the viewpoints of Stephen Mallarme, on the one hand, and T.S. Eliot, on the other, remains in the fact that, while Mallarme envisages a new kind of language, free from the rules of ordinary Grammar and Etymology, – language competent to evoke lofty feelings and emotions, Eliot holds the view that, superior realities can be touched with the help of ordinary language, provided the artist has the skill of locating suitable 'Objective Correlative' and creating a poetic texture through their combination.[4]

The very designation 'Objective Correlative' given to the factors that are responsible for the evocation of emotion in the mind of the reader indicates the two-fold pleasure, which, a specimen of poetic art, is required to cause to the connoisseur. The 'Objective Correlative' is a factor which makes an objective presentation of the emotive experience of the literary artist : the personal experience of the artist is given a universal form in this factor, as a result of which, when the reader makes himself acquainted with this objective unit, a similar emotion pertaining to his personal experience is evoked in his mind. The 'Objective Correlative', thus, universalises the particular experience of the artist, and when this is received by the reader, the universal experience boils down to the particular. In its aspect of objective presentation of the emotive experience, the evocating factor is 'Objective': in its aspect of arousing a similar emotion in the mind of the connoisseur, it is 'Correlative'. The 'Objective Correlative' is the universal symbol of a particular experience : at the same time, it evokes an emotion correlated with a similar emotion pertaining to the personal experience of the reader. As the experience is universal, the pleasure presented by it is sane and wholesome; as it particularises the universal at one stage, the pleasure donated by it is subjective and earthly.

An analysis of the concept of 'Objective Correlative' from this standpoint indicates that this is a bundle of irreconcilables. The Science of Literary Criticism itself believes that when a particular concept is described as creating reconciliation between opposites or as emerging as the habitat of contradictory qualities, what is intended to be signified or what actually emerges is that it is of transcendental character. It shows that such a concept is incapable of being adjudicated by applying the yard-stick of ordinary adjudication. In arriving at the concept of 'Objective Correlatives' or in making application of the pattern of Objective Correlative' to his poetic texture, Eliot betrays unmistakably the influence exerted on him by the French Symbolist Movement of Mallarme as also by the great master Aristotle. In his works entitled 'Physics',

'Metaphysics' and 'Rhetoric' Aristotle refers to three primordial elements of the soul. These elements are represented by, as Aristotle says, 'thumos', 'epithumos' and 'logistikon'. The 'thumos' tends to take the soul outside: it is rather centrifugal in character. The 'epithumos', on the other hand, tries to keep the soul confined within its own self; it avoids the pull of distraction and attachments for the external objects of enjoyment; it is centripetal in nature. The third element of the soul 'logistikon' is necessary for maintenance of harmony between the two contradictory qualities of 'thumos' and 'epithumos'. When this balance is established, the soul enjoys perfect repose and blissful condition of the soul emerges. The blissful state is referred to by the technical term 'liberation'. The liberation granted by Poetry, thus, is not emancipation in the sense to signify which it is employed in the treatises on philosophy: it is liberation from the exigency of the ordinary world, – attainment of a state where the soul enjoys bliss springing from a feeling of detachment-cum-involvement.[5] In poetry, the reader experiences universal emotion, as a result of which he is detached from the emotive experience presented in poetry; at the same time, he traces his own personal experience in the particular experience of the literary artist since universalised: and, therefore, he is involved to a great extent. This capacity of creating detachment and at the same time generating a sense of involvement in the mind of the connoisseur, who has done 'sufficient brain work' belonging to the 'Objective Correlative' goes to show again its transcendental nature.

T.S. Eliot believes in the principle that 'sufficient brain work' is necessary for the refined reader, who is to receive the specimen of literary art. This principle is in consistency with the conviction of Aristotle that, poetry demands a man with a special gift for its understanding, or rather one with a touch of madness in him. The former can easily get himself immersed in the required mood and the latter may be actually beside himself with that emotion. In making a distinction between the effects of Tragedy and Comedy in the mental plane of the reader and the spectator, Aristotle says that, Tragedy represents the best specimen of dramatic art, since it leads quickly to 'Catharsis'. By 'Catharsis' Aristotle refers to a blissful state of mind, in which the base feelings and ego-centred desires are purged, as a result of which, the soul reposes in its own self. Catharsis, therefore, is a state of liberation from considerations of small ego: in such a state the truncated ego disappears and the Grand and Big ego establishes itself, consequential upon which the reader is blissfully surprised to trace the heartbeat of the entire humanity in his own heart-beat. The 'Objective Correlative', as envisaged by Eliot, causes this catharsis, which is rather a disinterested experience of an emotion. Once again, the issue of disinterestedness appears and it is bound to appear and re-appear in poetry, because it constitutes the important criterion of Art as a whole. The 'Objective Correlative' is the objectified symbol of the emotion through employment of which the individual is converted into impersonal, -- involvement is transformed into disinterestedness. This is from the standpoint of creative process. When the process of appreciation of Poetry sets in, 'Objective Correlative' or the symbol is translated back into emotion, -- the universal into personal, disinterestedness into involvement. Such is the greatness of the Art of poetry, -- the greatness of the pattern created through employment of 'Objective Correlative', as envisaged by Eliot.

In describing the texture of Poetry, T.S. Eliot refers to the music of poetry, and maintains that versification plays a vital role in the matter of evocation of sentiment. Agreeing with Mallarme that the Poem must be received directly without questioning but always with fresh recognition, Eliot at the same time, says that words employed in poetry should not be such as make it impossible for the reader to ascertain the intention of the poet. It is for this reason that Eliot expresses the view that language of poetry cannot afford to lose its contact with the changing language of common intercourse.

Since words are the hardest material of Art being at the same time linguistic symbols as well as art symbols, Eliot advises the poets of posterity to take great care in regard to employment of words and to see that the efect of music is produced in the poem. Music represents the ideal Art symbol because musical-sound unlike the sound of words is completely bereft of the function of denotation: it functions as pure expression. While musical tissue is devoid of denotation, the poetic tissue is not; in a specimen of poetic art, the poet is required to employ words, which are significant ones, and which raise into comprehension both expressed and unexpressed meanings. This is why Eliot does not accept Mallarme's claim of the identity of poetry and music. He realises that in music the sound is of prime importance, but in poetry neither the sense can be sacrificed to the sound nor can the sound to the sense.[6]

Section II

Stand of Indian Aesthetics

It may be interesting at this point of time to have a look at the viewpoint of Indian Aesthetics on the means to be employed for the purpose of evocation of emotion in the mind of the experiencer in poetry. Indian Aesthetics considers emotive experience as the chief purpose of Poetic Art, and declares in unambiguous language the proposition that, 'Rasa' constitutes the be-all and end-all of poetry. The peculiar expression 'Rasa' is employed by Sanskrit Literary Theory to signify the state of Aesthetic Experience, springing from enjoyment of poetry. It is said that, when the permanent emotion, lying latent in the mind of the appreciator is called into play and the mind gets itself concentrated on reflection of that emotion, 'Rasa' manifests itself in its full splendour. To signify this permanent feeling, lying latent in the mind of the connoisseur in the form of a permanent disposition, Sanskrit Theory employs the term 'Sthayibhava'. This
thayibhava' is described as constituting the germ of Aes-
Experience: it is virtually the seed that sprouts in the
Rasa' or Aesthetic Experience in its total grandeur.

deavour to analyse the character of the perma-
ically known as the 'sthayibhava', Sanskrit
ake a psychological analysis of the

experiencer of a specimen of Poetic Art or all the forms of Art whatsoever, and arrives at certain permanent feelings, that reside in the minds of persons in the form of impressions. These feelings are shared by all men, irrespective of their difference in points of caste and creed, nationality and race, language and place of residence and time and circumstance of living. The permanent feeling resides in a subtle form, -- in the form of a latent impression in the minds of all persons; when the factors responsible for evocation of the permanent feeling appear, the permanent feeling is evoked, as a result of which the experiencer is pleased to have the delight of savouring his own emotion along with the emotions of others.

When the factors responsible for evocation of permanent feelings are withdrawn, the feeling also goes back to its dormant state, as a result of which, the experiencer is taken back to his normal state. The permanent feelings, therefore, are responsible for attainment of emotive experience, and consequently, they constitute the chief means of getting the splendid experience implanted into the mind of the connoisseur. Sanskrit Literary Theory asserts with all emphasis at its command that, the permanent feeling lying in the form of latent impression is the first pre-condition necessary for attainment of emotive experience, resulting from experience of poetry. The description of Visvanatha that the 'sthayibhava' constitutes the germ of Poetic Experience and that it is this permanent feeling that bloosoms forth in the form of 'Rasa', therefore, is surcharged with profound truth.[7]

Sanskrit Literary Theory asserts, further, that in order to have Aesthetic Experience it is necessary for the appreciator to have some sort of responsiveness, – the quality of identifying himself easily with the characters and situations presented in poetry, – the capability of sharing the emotive experience with all members of humanity. This capability which reminds one of the concept of 'sufficient brain-work' as projected by T.S. Eliot, is referred to by Sanskrit Theory through the expression 'Sahridayata', that is to say, 'aesthetic sensibility'. In explaining 'aesthetic sensibility', which resides in the real connoisseur of Poetic Art alone,

Abhinavagupta says that, a connoisseur is one who makes himself acquainted with literary creations of all master artists, as a result of which whose mind becomes soft and full of responsiveness to the chain of events, set of objects, characters and emotions presented in the specimen of poetic art. Such a connoisseur, it is said, is a like-hearted friend of the literary artist: he does not see the literary artist or his product from a distance: on the other hand, he knows how to identify himself with the artist and his creation; this means that he is one with the poet. This quality of 'aesthetic sensibility' is the essential condition necessary for attainment of emotive experience : as a matter of fact, it enables the labour put by the literary artist in carving out poetical paintings to fulfil its purpose : without this the effort of the artist remains unfulfilled and unfructified. Visvanatha categorically states that, Aesthetic Experience is not caused without the latent impression and the quality of 'aesthetic sensibility'. In his endeavour to justify this statement, he points out that, the very fact that, the *dried* Vedic scholars and the unresponsive grammarians are unable to react in the desired manner to poetry and music, performing art and painting shows that they are devoid of this sensibility: the fact, on the other hand, that the cultured and refined connoisseur, who have experienced play of feelings in their minds are in a position to derive aesthetic experience shows that they are endowed with this aesthetic sensibility. All these, Visvanatha says, show that aesthetic sensibility is a factor essential to attainment of Aesthetic Experience. Without it, aesthetic experience is not derived : it remains a dream, incapable of being brought into consummation in the empirical plane.[8] When the concept of 'sthayibhava', as projected by Sanskrit Literary Theory is combined with the concept of 'sahridayata' or 'aesthetic sensibility', the principle that the permanent feeling is not the 'brute emotion', but rather the 'refined form of emotion' emerges. Sanskrit theory subscribes to the opinion that, the 'sthayibhava' is not the 'raw feeling' or simple 'animal instinct' remaining in the mind of the experiencer, but rather a superior form of it, attained through a continuous process of cultural refinement. The 'sthayibhava', therefore, is not simply the permanent feeling residing in the form of latent impression, but the permanent feeling to which a superior form has been given by a continuous process of socio-cultural refinement. It is affirmed that, only those appreciators, who are endowed with the permanent refined feeling, lying in the form of latent disposition and aesthetic sensibility are in a position to attain Aesthetic Experience. In support of this observation, Visvanatha cites a statement of Dharmadatta which says that only appreciators, endowed with impressions and aesthetic sensibilities are in a position to experience and enjoy poetry; appreciators devoid of permanent impressions and aesthetic instincts, on the other hand, are exactly like the inanimate pillars and seats in the auditorium: just as the inanimate objects stored in the stage or the auditorium do not have any aesthetic experience, similarly such persons devoid of aesthetic instincts and impressions also do not have any blissful enjoyment. The permanent feeling and aesthetic sensibility, thus, constitute the chief internal ingredients necessary for appreciation of Poetry. These are internal to the connoisseur. To evoke this permanent feeling lying latent in the form of impression in the mind of appreciator it becomes necessary for the poet to create poetical paintings, presenting characters and situations, set of objects and chain of events. Sanskrit Literary Theory takes note of this principle, and asserts that objective presentation of characters and situations, set of objects and chain of events is necessary to effect evocation of emotive experience. To signify this means of objective presentation, which, in their turn, effect evocation of emotive experience Sanskrit Literary Theory employs three technical terms, – the 'Vibhava', the 'Anubhava' and the 'Sancaribhava'.[9]

In its attempt to explain the nature of the 'Vibhava', the 'Anubhava' and the 'Sancaribhava' or the 'Vyabhicaribhava', Sanskrit Literary Theory states that, when the causes and effects of ordinary emotions are presented in poetry through medium of expression, they acquire a different status and special designations are employed to signify them. In a similar manner, the feelings that accompany permanent moods, when presented through the medium of poetry attain a special status and form, and consequently a fresh designation is employed to signify them. Thus the actual lady Parvati is the cause of evocation of feeling in the mind of Lord Siva; when she is represented in poetry through medium of expression and is converted into a universal symbol she no longer remains an ordinary cause. Sanskrit Literary Theory notes this process of transformation of the ordinary character into an extra-ordinary universal factor responsible for evocation of emotive experience in the mind of the connoisseur and employs the novel expression 'Vibhava' to signify it. The 'Vibhava', thus, is the universal symbol of the cause working behind evocation of emotive experience in the mind of the reader.

The same process happens in the case of 'Anubhava' which is the universalised effect of ordinary emotion, presented through the medium of Poetry. When the feeling of love is generated in the mind, it gets expression through certain movements, physical changes and utterances of the person concerned; when these physical-cum-psychic changes are presented through medium of expression, they get universal status, and play significant role in the matter of evocation of emotive experience in the mind of the appreciator. The ordinary physical and psychic changes tracable in the particular man is the common effect of love; the objectified presentation of these physical and spiritualistic changes through the medium of poetry receives a universal status, as a result of which, the ordinary cause-and-effect-theory is not applicable in their case. It is for this reason that Sanskrit Literary Theory employs a special term 'Anubhava' to signify these effects of manifestation of permanent feelings.

The proposition that the ordinary Cause-and-Effect-Theory is not applicable in the case of the 'Vibhava' and the 'Anubhava' takes the curious critic to the gateway of the deeper principle, -- the principle relating to 'Poetic Indealisation'. In his endeavour to explain the significance of the peculiar designations 'Vibhava' and 'Anubhava', Visvanatha says that, both these factors do have a peculiar power of universalization, as a result of which they shake off their particularities and appear as universal symbols of exciting factors and ensuent effects of permanent feelings. Since the characters, the set of objects, the chain of events and the physical and psychic changes noticable in the original personages become endowed with the capacity of being converted into 'Universal Symbols' when projected through the medium of expression in poetry, they, in their turn, generate universal emotive experience in the mind of the connoisseur, who does not experience any difficulty in identifying himself with the characters and situations, set of objects and chain of events projected in poetry. The particularity of the reader is put into slumber; he is conducted to a universal plane, as a result of which the chain of events that appear as absurd and inappropriate in the case of an ordinary man do not appear absurd and inoperative in his case. With all emphasis at his command, Visvanatha predicates the existence of this capacity to universalize in regard to the 'Vibhava' and the 'Anubhava', and in explaining the peculiar nature of these two factors says that, when the refined reader makes himself acquainted with the characters and situations, the chain of events and series of effects, these are accepted by him neither as strictly belonging to another, nor as not belonging to another, -- neither as related directly to his own self, nor as having no relation with himself; this, indeed, is a peculiar state of mind in which individuality and particularity play no role, whatsoever. All these show that the emotive experience generated from appreciation of poetry is not limited by any sense of individuality or particularity: it is characterised by universality, as a result of which it becomes possible for the refined reader to experience it in its total grandeur. As the emotive experience is universal in character, so the causes and effects of this experience also are universal in their nature. The creation of the literary artist, Sanskrit Literary Theory says, is universal in the sense that, it becomes possible for the universal man to identify himself with the characters and situations, the chain of events and the series of effects; it does not mean that like scientific knowledge it is an abstract entity. Characters and situations, projected by the literary artist through the medium of poetic expression is not a symbol outline devoid of colour and form; rather it is an objectified concrete entity. In this objectified presentation of the chain of events and the series of effects, presentation of feelings and their ensuents, that the community of connoisseurs finds itself reflected. Sanskrit Literary Theory, thus, arrives at the conclusion that, the poetic creation is a creation of "Concrete Universal"; it is the objectified presentation of the chain of events and series of objects, situations and circumstances, that are responsible for transformation of the ordinary particular into the concrete universal. When ordinary causes and effects acquire special forms and become responsible for genesis of "Concrete Universal", they are regarded as the 'Vibhava' and 'Anubhava' in the terminology of Sanskrit Literary Theory.[10]

Continuing his discussion on principles relating to structuring of the plot and finding out its relation with the emotive experience, Anandavardhana says that, the different stages in the development of the plot are to be indicated in such a way that, these become helpful to evocation of emotive experience in the mind of the appreciator. He pronounces a note of caution to the effect that, the different stages and the junctures should not be incorporated according to the dictates of Literary Criticism alone. Thirdly, the emotion at hand is to be evoked at times, and at times care should be taken to see that it gets subdued maintaining, at the same time, a small under-current within. It is necessary for the literary artist to introduce variety in his literary creation through presentation of emotive experience of different types, but in all such cases, while predominance of one emotional mood is to be retained, others are to be presented in such a way that, they become able to maintain their subservience throughout the work. The poetic figures and literary embellishments are to be incorporated keeping an eye on the part played by them in the matter of evocation of emotive experience, that constitutes the chief objective of Literary Art. With all emphasis at his command, Anandavardhana says that, even if the literary artist is endowed with profound genius and is able to incorporate shining literary embellishments in his poetic texture, these instruments of decoration are to be applied by considering their capability of raising the emotive experience into comprehension. In the view of Anandavardhana, a plot structured according to the abovenoted five principles becomes able to evoke emotive experience in the mind of the connoisseur and consequently, proves itself organically related to the Literary Art itself.

The relation which the plot bears to the emotive experience is absoloutely clear. The goal of poetry is represented by emotive experience or 'Rasa'; and every effort is to be taken by the poet to structure the plot and incorporate the excitant and ensuent, the chain of objects and series of events in such a way that, they become helpful to evocation of emotive experience. In this connexion, Anandavardhana introduces the issue of antimony of emotions, and asserts that incorporation of excitants and ensuents, chain of objects and series of events connected with an emotional mood, that is opposed to the main emotional mood often mars the beauty of Poetic Art, and consequently, such depiction is to be avoided. In his endeavour to find out other factors which lead to breach of 'Rasa' or prove themselves detrimental to attainment of Aesthetic Experience, Anandavardhana describes a few more cases where this happens, and the specimen of poetic art becomes unable to fulfil its objective. Such a situation is created when the literary artist introduces another series of objects or chain of events related to a new emotion, when the series of objects and chain of events at hand have made considerable progress in effecting evocation of the intended emotive experience. A similar situation is created when the excitants and the ensuents, the series of objects and chain of events are withdrawn at a time when they should have been exhibited in their full form or these are exhibited in detail at a time when they ought to have been withdrawn. The fourth situation is created when the highly developed emotive experience is allowed to be revealed again and again, making the emotive experience itself stale through constant exhibition. Anandavardhana warns that, such situations are to be avoided in order to keep the specimen of poetic art free from the blemish that proves itself detrimental to evocation of emotive experience. Summing up his observations on the linkage which the plot is supposed to bear to the emotive experience, Anandavardhana says that, the rules indicated by him may be taken as samples or specimens, and fresh norms may be evolved by literary artists in their endeavour to make the plot organically related to the emotive experience, constituting the essence of Poetic Art itself. The firm declaration of Anandavardhana is this that, depiction of a plot, containing excitants and ensuents, permanent and transient feelings, chain of objects and series of events not related to the emotive experience shows the lack of poetic genius on the part of the literary artist, and consequently, structuring of such a plot is to be avoided with meticulous care. In this connexion, Anandavardhana refers to certain situations created by such stalwarts like Kalidasa and Vyasa and says that, though in structuring their plots and handling them, such great poets have created certain undesirable situations and introduced in-appropriate chains of events and series of objects, yet they have been able to prevent the degeneration of literary art by taking recourse to certain other devices with the help of their profound poetic genius. The norms indicated by Anandavardhana, therefore, are norms meant for adoption by ordinary literary artists struggling to transplant the emotive experience into the mind of the connoisseur. Great poets like Vyasa, Valmiki and Kalidasa are to evolve their own norms, because greatness does not keep itself confined within the limits imposed by ordinary norms and stale rules.[11]

In his attempt to explain the capability of the 'Vibhava' to universalise a symbol, Visvanatha cites a statement of Bhartrihari, the great Grammarian-Philosopher, who admits a special function belonging to the expression. Bhartrihari expresses the opinion that when characters and situations constitute the content of comprehension being expressed through the medium of expression, they attain an existential status and at the same time appear as generalised situations and characters, divested of particularities. This particular aspect of comprehension, it is said, differentiates it from other means of comprehension, like the Perception, the Inference and the Analogy. In the view of Bhartrihari, therefore, the expression has two-fold purpose: on the one hand, it gives an existential status to series of events and chain of objects, – to characters and situations and present them as vividly or even more vididly, as other means of cognition, like Perception and Inference: on the other hand, it converts particular chain of events and series of objects, – particular characters and situations to their universalised forms. Sanskrit Literary Theory, that draws support frequently from speculations of the Science of Language says that when ordinary expression is endowed with this capability of signifying generalised ideas and universalised concepts, it is no wonder that the poetic expression acquires this capability of signifying universalised notions in a higher degree. The poetic expression differs from the ordinary expression in respect of the complete merger between the language and meaning, as also in point of the harmony and balance that is established between the charm of expression and charm of content. It is this splendid harmony between the charming expression and enchanting content, – the character of the poetic texture and the nature of the poetic meaning that distinguishes poetic expression from ordinary linguistic expression and invests the former with a greater power of presenting a universal symbol.[12]

Visvanatha extends recognition to two types of 'Vibhava': the 'Alambana' and the 'Uddipana'. This is just a re-statement of the traditional view of the Indian Aesthetics, – of the theory enunciated by the literary theoreticians. These theoreticians attempt this two-fold classification of the 'Vibhava': the 'Alambana', it is said, is represented by the characters like the hero and the heroine, because they constitute the locus of the main emotional mood. The 'Uddipana', on the other hand, is represented by situations and circumstances, as also by the actions and movements of the characters, because they excite the permanent feeling belonging to the original personage. Thus 'Parvati' as presented by Kalidasa constitutes the 'Alambana', while her movements and gestures, as also the advent of spring in the penance-grove constitute the 'Uddipana'. It is to be noted, however, that these are raised to the status of 'Alambana' and 'Uddipana' only when they are presented through the medium of the poetic expression.

Sanskrit Literary Theory enunciates in details the principle with regard to unfolding of the plot, as also the norms that are to be adopted by the literary artists in the matter of presentation of characters and situations, -- chain of events and series of objects. Anandavardhana considers 'Rasa' as constituting the centre of gravity of Poetic Art, and continues to say that the plot is to be planned and handled in such a way that 'Rasa' is able to manifest itself in its full splendour. As regards the way in which the plot is to be planned and handled, Anandavardhana enunciates a five-point formula, which is to be adopted by the artist aiming to achieve lasting fame. Firstly, the 'Vibhava', the 'Alambana', etc., or in other words, characters and situations, excitants and ensuents, permanent and transient feelings appropriate to the emotions intended to be delineated are to be symbolised: neither the characters, the situations, the permanent feelings and transient ones should be in excess of the emotive experience intended to be presented nor they should fall short of the emotive experience at hand. This means that the excitants and ensuents, the permanent and transient feelings are to be absolutely appropriate to the emotive experience intended to be transplanted into the minds of the connoisseurs. Elaborating this principle, Anandavardhana says that, while divine gestures are to be incorporated in respect of divine characters, human behaviours are to be delineated in case of characters that are strictly human in nature. Anandavardhana feels that if actions and passions, common to ordinary man, are predicated in regard to divine personages or divine actions and passions are predicted in regard to ordinary persons, the specimen of literary art becomes vitiated by the defect of inappropriateness, which cuts at the roots of attainment of Aesthetic Experience itself. When such characters, however, are chosen that possess both human and divine passions and actions, the author is free to present divine or human passions and actions in regard to them. It is possibly for this reason that Bharata tenders advice to poets and dramatists of posterity to choose as the themes of their works, such plots, the emotive experience of which is determined beforehand. Anandavardhana pronounces a note of caution here, and tenders advice to posterity not to introduce any such modification in the plot that may endanger the quality of the emotive experience intended to be predominently presented in the Poetry. In explaining the Poetry, the emotive experience of which is fixed, Anandavardhana says that, it refers to that Poem, which has attained such celebrity that as soon as the connoisseur takes note of the fact that, the Poem is based on that particular plot, he starts attaining aesthetic experience, without depending in any way on the plot presented by the literary artist. This means that the main melody of the plot is established and extremely common: the reader does not stand in necessity of following the development of the plot as treated by the new author in order to attain splendid emotive experience.[13]

Continuing his argument that the sole determining factor in regard to designing and handling of the plot as also the form of poetic texture is represented by the principle of 'Propriety' or Appropriateness, Anandavardhana develops four other norms in regard to incorporation of characters and situations, chain of events and series of objects, permanent and transient feelings. Thus, he says if the plot chosen by the poet contain certain incidents that are not favourable to evocation of emotive experience, but rather are detrimental to it, these are to be avoided and such new incidents planned, as may evoke the intended emotive experience in the mind of the connoisseur. The literary artist has for his chief objective transplantation of emotive experience, and only such expressions and contents are to be incorporated as are in a position to effect transplantation of experience and fulfil the objective of the artist. In this connexion Sri Atul Gupta raises an interesting issue in regard to the plot of the Ramayana. He refers to the controversy that was very much in vogue in the forties in regard to the competence of the new literary artist to incorporate changes in the plot of the Ramayana and says that, while one section of scholars admit this right, other section holds the firm view that as Rama is extolled as a divine personage the literary artist does not have the right to paint his character in such a way that the religious sentiment of the reader gets affected. Sri Gupta makes it clear that, this controversy is useless, because the land of Poetry is a completely different kind of land, -- different from that constituting the area of religion. In realm of Poetry there is only one principle, -- the principle of Propriety, -- the principle of Appropriateness to the emotive experience. This principle of propriety does not regulate society nor does it guide religious precepts and practices.

Section III

Music & Meaning

T.S. Eliot attaches great importance to the music in poetry and affirms that a perfect system of music is as much necessary as the grand nature of the meaning for evocation of emotive experience in the mind of the connoisseur. This means that the literary artist is required to master the art of handling rhythm and metre in the specimen of literary art, so much so that the language of the poem itself becomes able to generate emotive experience corresponding to that of the literary artist in the mind of the appreciator. So far as this capability to handle rhythm and metre in the proper way is concerned, Eliot says that, the accepted rules of scansion or a close study of Metrics does not help the artist in any way in locating the metre and rhyme suitable for evocation of the emotive experience, intended to be transplanted by him in the particular document of literary art. He compares the study of Metrics with the study of Anatomy, and says that just as the study of Anatomy does not teach how to make a hen lay eggs, similarly an examination of the rules of prosody does not make a literary artist create specimen of literary art, enchanting by the flow of superb music.

In his endeavour to identify the factor which lies beyond location of metres and rhymes suitable to evocation of particular emotive experience, Eliot arrives at the study of metrical compositions that can train the ears and imitation of great literary artists who have gifted certain grand musical poems to humanity. When Eliot speaks of imitation he does not refer simply to the cold-blooded imitation of a style of a particular literary artist, but to the deeper imitation of the mind of the artist, which is responsible for the genesis of metrical compositions, rendered enchanting by flow of flawless music. The cold-blooded imitation leads to disenchantments, while imitation of the mind, -- of the bigger personality projected in the grand documents of literary art creates a new enchantment for the poetry created by the junior artist, who lays his hands upon this bigger imitation. Eliot, therefore, encourages deeper imitation, -- imitation of the bigger personality, which is something distinct from imitation of the style, peculiar to the truncated individuality of the great artist.

The position becomes all the more confused by admixture of diverse influences in versification employed in a peculiar literature. The English verse, as a matter of fact, has been influenced to a great extent by the native metres of Latin poetry, which is more accentual than syllabic corresponding to the Vedic metre. It bears influence further of the Greek metre which also is more accentual than syllabic. In this connection T.S. Eliot refers to Homer and Vergil, and says that to the audience of the age of Vergil, pleasure in the poetry arose from the presence in it of two metrical schemes. This presence of two schemes in a particular document of literary art makes the situation complicated, but at the same time it lends enchantment to the document under consideration.

In trying to identify the rhythms that have executed profound influence on the rhythms of English Poetry, Eliot refers further to the rhythms of the Anglo-Saxon, Celtic, Norman, French, of middle English and Scots, as also to the rhythms of Latin, and, at various periods of French, Italian and Spanish. English rhythm, thus, is comparable to an amalgam of races, where the admixture of the components of different races leads to the genesis of one race. In this connection, Eliot maintains that, as in human beings in a composite race, different strains are dominant in different individuals, similarly in the realm of poetry different strains may be dominant in different poems and poets; but in spite of these differences one thing remains and this is that poetry is to retain its close connection with ordinary everyday language which the reader is accustomed to use and hear. Poetry, thus, is required to be composed in ordinary everyday language or in other words, the materials for construction of poetical paintings are furnished by words employed in everyday language. This is possibly the reason why the contemporary poetry gives the connoisseur an astounding feeling of excitement and a deeper sense of fulfilment different from the sentiment aroused by even very much greater poetry of a past age.[14] T.S. Eliot, thus, advocates employment of ordinary language in the realm of Poetic Art, and in this respect he differs from the obscure French writer Stephen Mallarme, who favours the idea of employment of a special type of language in poetry. Mallarme makes up a language, which is entirely his own by a refined choice of words and by using exceptional turns of speech; he maintains that, in order to remain faithful to the inner language of form, literary artist must invent words and create images, - he must mishandle and stretch the meaning of words.

T.S. Eliot understands the danger that lies latent in this proposition of Mallarme. The danger here is that the words may be so strange that, recognition of the poet's intention may become totally impossible. He, therefore, refers to the non-sense verse of Edward Lear, which, unfortunately, in spite of being a parody of sense does not scale the height of poetic intensity. According to Eliot, Edward Lear's non-sense is not 'vacuity of sense', but rather a 'parody of sense', and that is the sense of it: *The Jumblies* is a poem of adventure, -- and of nostalgia for romance of foreign voyage and exploration.

The *Yongy-Bongy-Bo* and *The Dong with Lumious Nose* are poems of unrequitted passion -- blues in fact. The music, that is of high order is definitely enjoyed, and at the same time what appears amusing is the feeling of irresponsibility towards sense. There may be such types of poems in which the connoisseur may be moved by the music and take the sense for granted, but this cannot reach the height arrived at by the sublime poetry. A document of literary art is to possess the enchantment of both music and meaning, and since meaning becomes all the more clear when ordinary everyday language is employed in poetry, Eliot advocates the proposition of carving out poetical paintings with the help of ordinary words employed in everyday language. And Eliot's proposition is not merely the proposition of employment of ordinary language, but at the same time, the proposition of an amalgam of enchantment of music and charmingness of meaning, because as he says, 'music of poetry is not something, which exists apart from the meaning'.[15]

In his eagerness to show that an amalgam of a musical pattern of sound and a musical pattern of meaning is essential for blossoming forth of grand and sublime poetry, T.S. Eliot introduces the theory in regard to different interpretations merging from the same poetic expression, or for the matter of fact, the whole specimen of poetic art. So far as the meaning of a document of literary art is concerned, it varies from reader to reader, and all these different types of meaning may not necessarily be identical with the meaning to signify which the poetry is constructed by the literary artist. Meaning, after all is not just the paraphrase and it is possible that, the meaning of a poem may wholly escape paraphrasing. In this connection Eliot refers to English translation of Stephen Mallarme's Poems by Roger Fry and says that though the English translation brings into light the inspiration that lies behind the construction of poetical paintings, it is not in a position to present the real meaning of the poems.

The reason is simple; the paraphrase can convey only a part of the meaning but never the total meaning. This possibly happens because the meaning has its linkage with the Infinite; the poet is occupied with the frontiers of consciousness beyond which his words fail but meanings continue to exist. In elaborating this point, Eliot proceeds further to say that, the literary artist creates certain symbols competent to give expression to his personal experience, that is unrelated to something outside; when this symbol is grasped properly by the connoisseur, it becomes the expression of a general situation and at the same time it gives rise to emergence of a private experience in his mind. As the nature of private experience differs from man to man, so the nature of meaning congnizable to connoisseurs also differs from reader to reader. By asserting that the meaning of a poem differs from the reader to reader and that a specimen of literary art may convey a meaning, which is something different from the meaning to signify which the poetical painting is carved out and consequently is something remote from its origin, Eliot gives a vast area to the poetic meaning and takes the curious reader to the doorway of the Theory that while the meaning of an ordinary expression has got a fixed form, the meaning of a poetic expression is vast, varied and unlimited.[16]

Though Eliot attaches so much importance to the component of meaning, he is, nevertheless, aware of the significant role played by the sound-element, and because of this, in his numerous critical essays, he expresses the view that, poetry should be constructed with the help of ordinary everyday language, so that the reader can easily understand the relation of the document of literary art with the speech of his time. It is not without reason, therefore, that Wordsworth had to announce in his preface to the Lyrical Ballads that, poetry should stage a return to common speech. The same truth had been asserted one century earlier by Oldham, Waller, Denham and Dryden. All these mean that whenever in moments of history, literary artists have rejected the ordinary common language, -- the current speech of their time and surroundings, a caution has been pronounced to return to the common speech, -- the ordinary language. It is, of course, to be remembered that no poetry "is ever exactly the same speech that the poet talks and hears; but it has to be in such a relation to the speech of his time that the listener or reader can say that this is the best contemporary poetry and that this is how I should talk if I could talk poetry." The brilliant specimen of Poetic Art, thus, bears close linkage to the speech of the time of the literary artist and the listener, and this is the reason why contemporary poetry gives us a feeling of excitement and a sense of general fulfilment, which is incapable of being given by the greatest poetry of the past.

It is interesting to note that though T.S. Eliot advocates the amalgam of the aura of words and enchantment of meanings, there are critics who put greater emphasis on the variety of verbal sounds, -- the musical sounds, that are devoid of the function of pure expression. Walter De La Mare maintains the view that, the intrinsic suggestive quality of words is changed due to their position, and that the quality, the volume, the pitch and the intonation of the words are responsible to a great extent for presentation of different types of meanings. In his work *The Logical Syntax of Language* Rudolph Carnap analyses the concept of linguistic symbols and tries to draw the line of demarcation between the linguistic symbol and the aesthetic symbol and writes: "many linguistic utterances are analogous to laughing in that, they have only an expressive function, no representative function. Examples of these are cries like 'Oh Oh', or, on a higher level, lyrical verse. The aim of a lyrical poem in which occur the words 'sun-shine' and' clouds' is not to inform us of certain meteorological facts, but to express certain feelings of the poet and to excite similar feeling in us." It is believed by some that if poetry has favoured the way of the ear and has given itself jealously to the tuneful ordering of sounds, it is because sense was conveyed by sounds before words were invented and this primitive power still survives in sounds as well as in letters. This view is expressed by Wordsworth, Dryden and Mallarme, as also by Sir Walter Raleigh, apart from Paul Valery and Stephen Mallarme, who postulate the theory in regard to employment of a different type of speech for the purpose of construction of the poetical creation.[17] An analysis of the experience of the refined reader, however, shows that if the meanings of words are ignored and too much importance is placed on the music of the sound of words, the poetry becomes feeble to work and evoke emotive experience in the connoisseur. When the meaning is understood, the musical quality of the words acquires a new significance, and the result that is produced in the shape of evocation of emotive experience turns out to be splendid. It is, therefore, clear that the meaning of words cannot be taken in isolation from the musical quality of the words nor can the music of the sound or words be taken in isolation from the enchantment of meaning. It is for this reason that Eliot projects the Theory in regard to the amalgam of the musical pattern of sound and the musical pattern of meaning. In his theory a "Musical Poem" is a poem, which has a musical pattern of sound and a musical pattern of secondary meanings of the words, which compose it and that these two patterns are indissoluble and one. Since the musical quality of the word has its own role to play in the matter of evocation of emotive experience, Eliot expresses the view that, it may be profitable for the poet to devote himself to the study of music, – not to its technicalities, but rhythms and metres, so that a sense of rhythm and a sense of structure can develop in the literary artist. When these two senses develop in the poet, it becomes possible for him to locate the particular rhythm of the particular poem before the specimen of literary art can actually find expression in words. It is this location of rhythm that becomes greatly helpful in the task of genesis of the idea and image. Thus while most of the literary theoreticians speak of the importance either of the musical quality of the sound or enchantment of the meaning, Eliot recognises the importance of both, and asserts that neither the aura of words can be used in isolation from the hallow of meanings nor can the aura of meanings separated from the hallow of words. While other literary theoreticians speak of the movement of the literary artist from the idea to the image and the literary symbol, because as they say, the mind of the poet remains absorbed in contemplation of emotion and the literary symbol rushes forth spontaneously from his heart, Eliot projects the theory that, the rhythm is located even before the poem reaches expression and that once the rhythm is located, it becomes easy for the poet to locate the idea and the image. In the view of T.S. Eliot the sound and the sense are inseparable, and the musical poem is an amalgam of the musical pattern of sound and the musical pattern of sense. This theory of equal importance of the sound and the sense and the fusion of the two patterns in the Sublime Poetry, reminds the curious reader naturally of the views expressed by Sanskrit Poetics on this fundamental issue.

It may be profitable at this point of time to discuss the point of view of Sanskrit Poetics on the problem of imitation, nature of the implied meaning and the harmonious blending between the music of poetry and music of meaning. So far as the problem of imitation is concerned, Sanskrit Poetics tenders advice to budding poets to imitate the styles of established literary artists, apart from having a deep penetration into their works, a penetration that can train the ear. Before analysing the different types of imitation, Ksemendra, the noted literary critic of the eleventh century A.D., advises the new literary artists to receive instructions in the Art of Poetry from literary artists endowed with creative genius, because as he says, selection of a cold logician or an insipid grammarian as the trainer is likely to endanger the process of genesis of poetic expression itself. He tenders further advice to get oneself acquainted not only with the composition of master-artists, and the science of Metrics in all its details, but to have a first-hand knowledge of the ordinary spoken language of the masses and different dialects that emerge in different places, so that the poetry remains able to maintain its linkage with common and ordinary speech. This advice tendered by Ksemendra exhibits the view of Sanskrit Poetics that, the poet is required to study the classification of metres and pay proper respect to the accepted rules of scansion, because only conformity to these rules can infuse music into a specimen of Poetic Art. It also projects in a succint manner the theory of Sanskrit Poetics that, in order to be attractive Poetry is required to remain close to ordinary everyday language, which we use and hear, because when the Poetry loses its contact with language of common intercourse its enchantment becomes lost.[18]

Ksemendra leaves a long note on different types of imitation, that are to be followed by a beginner in his endeavour to attain maturity, pronouncing a note of caution all the time that, this is to be adopted under the guidance of a mature literary artist, endowed with profound creative genius. The first type of imitation consists in imitation of content, which is expressed through the medium of a totally different expression. The second consists in employment of a few words employed in a grand specimen of Poetic Art, so that the hand becomes trained in inducting suitable expressions, fitted to the expressions employed earlier by a great poet. The third type of imitation consists in creation of three new feet, keeping one feet employed by a literary artist of repute intact. There are other types of imitation, also, which are to be practised by the poet, so that he can acquire mastery over the art of metres and induct a grand musical pattern into his literary creation. While all these types of imitation are adored and consequently recommended for the budding artist, the best type of imitation, Ksemendra asserts, is represented by the deeper imitation, -- the imitation of the spirit of the profound artist. The profound artist, in his turn, Ksemendra continues, is in a position to reflect the mind of the nation, -- the mind that continues for all time to come and reveals itself in its full glory through all literary and cultural activities of the nation. Vyasa, Ksemendra proclaims, adopted this type of imitation : he could catch the mind of the nation and give expression to the spirit of India in his works : this explains the greatness of Vyasa, as also the attempt made by subsequent literary artists to draw materials and even imagaries from the literary creation of Vyasa.[19]

Sanskrit Poetics accepts the position that the implied meaning differs from the explicit meaning not only from the point of view of form, but also from the point of view of number and cause of comprehension. In his endeavour to establish the proposition that, the implicit differs from the explicit, and consequently is a profound verity, Anandavardhana advances a number of arguments supported by illustrations, taken mostly from verses composed in ordinary conversational language of the village folk. The very fact that Anandavardhana chooses the language of common intercourse as the medium of communication or selects such verses as are composed in language of common intercourse shows that, in the view of this great literary critic, poetry is to maintain its connexion with ordinary everyday language which we use and hear.

One of the arguments furnished by Anandavardhana in this connexion consists in the fact that the explicit differs from the implicit in point of number. And this is so, because the explicit is directly communicated through expression, and consequently is fixed in nature. The implicit, however, differs from person to person, and consequently, is characterised by multiplicity. The literary artist employs a poetic expression to signify a particular meaning, linked with his personal experience : when this expression is caught by the refined reader, it evokes different experiences in the mind of the reader, -- different from that of the literary artist, as also different from that of others. This means that a poem is in a position to mean different meanings to different readers, and all these meanings may be absolutely different from what the author thought he meant. The peculiarity of the poetic expression lies in this capability of the expression to raise into comprehension different implicit meanings, according to difference in levels of consciousness of the appreciator. The literary artist remains absorbed on the contemplation of his personal emotive experience; to give expression to this experience he employs expression. The expression, therefore, reaches the frontiers of consciousness of the artist; beyond the limits of this consciousness it is unable to move. The meaning, however, being infinite in nature is in a position to travel beyond the frontiers of consciousness of the artist. And this is so, because the level of consciousness differs from literary artist to refined reader and from one refined reader to another appreciative connoisseur. It is not without reason, therefore, that, Sanskrit Literary theory repeatedly proclaims that sufficient 'brain work' is necessary, not only for construction of poetical paintings, but also for their appreciation. When the document of literary art is experienced by a real connoisseur, it shakes the roots of his consciousness, so to say, and consequently, a new meaning emerges depending on the range of his consciousness. Impression differs from man to man and consciousness differs from connoisseur to connoisseur. The Sanskrit Literary Theory therefore, proclaims that the meaning of a Poetry differs from reader to reader. This meaning, in its turn, is in a position to differ from that intended to be conveyed by the literary artist. The plain and simple truth is that with reference to Poetry there is no last word; nobody can say that this is the meaning of the Poem.[20]

So far as the question of relative importance of sound or meaning is concerned, Sanskrit Literary Theory holds the view that the issue is rather immaterial, inasmuch as, the relation between the two is inseparable in Poetry and there is a perfect compound of the music of sound and the musical pattern of sense in a great and grand specimen of poetic art. In his endeavour to describe Poetry, Kuntaka, a literary theoretician of 11th century A.D. states that, poetry is presented by an inseparable compound of sound and sense, -- an inseparable association of the musical pattern of sound and the musical pattern of sense. Kuntaka means to say that the charmingness belongs to the music of the sound as also to the music of the sense, and in his endeavour to bring home the point that the enchantment of Poetry owes its genesis to the charm of every sound and every sense, as also to the charm of the peculiar combination of the two, he introduces the parallelism of the oil residing in each and every particle of sesame. It is said that just as oil resides in every grain, similarly enchantment of Poetry resides in each and every ingredient of the poetic painting, -- the ingredients represented by the sound, the sense and the perfect amalgam of the musical pattern of sound and the musical pattern of sense.

Expanding this dictum of perfect amalgam of sound and sense, – of the indissoluble amalgam of the musical pattern of sound and the musical pattern of sense, Kuntaka proceeds to say that the poetic expression is that expression which alone is in a position to signify the intended idea of the Poet, – to evoke an emotive experience similar to that of the literary artist in the mind of the connoisseur. The poetic meaning similarly is the meaning which is enchanting by its own nature, so much so that the reader, possessed of appreciative genius becomes able to trace his own emotive experience in the experience symbolised in Poetry, and consequently is in a position to savour supramundane delight. Since the poetic expression and the poetic meaning, both are enchanting by their very nature, the question as to whether the specimen of literary art owes its charmingness to the sense or to the sound is immaterial. Kuntaka firmly asserts the view that, the combination of embellished sound and ornamented sense, – the musical pattern of sound and the musical pattern of meaning, so to say, constitutes Poetry, and consequently it is a mis-statement to say that, the poetic figures belong to the texture of Poetry: the real position is that the texture of Poetry is represented by embellished word and meaning, and the musical sound and sense.[21]

The theory adumbrated by Kuntaka gets its start at the hands of Anandavardhana, who projects, for the first time, the theory in regard to the joint action of the word and meaning in the matter of suggesting the symbolic. Anandavardhana states that, the inexplicably charming symbolic is neither raised into comprehension by sound alone nor by sense alone, but rather by both the sound and the sense acting together, implying thereby that, it is as much necessary to enter into the core of the explicit meaning as is to appreciate the aura of sound.

In furnishing a definition of the best specimen of Poetic Art, which is technically known as 'Dhvani', Anandavardhana says that, in this specimen of Poetic Art, the expression renders its explicit meaning subservient and the explicit meaning also makes its own self subordinate, and the two conjointly go to raise into comprehension the symbolic content of inexplicable charm. Though the expression and the explicit conjointly suggest the symbolic, there exists a difference in the importance of the role of the two, and this explains the different designations applied to the diverse types of the best specimen of Poetic Art or 'Dhvani', like that based on sound and that based on sense, and so on and so on.

Anandavardhana expresses the opinion that aesthetic experience is caused not only by Poems signifying explicit meanings, but also by music and musical movement of limbs. In such cases, the search after the explicit meaning fails, because the musical notes are unable to signify any meaning with the help of the function of Denotation. These notes, however, bear close linkage to particular emotions and emotive experiences, as a result of which as soon as they are listened, they give rise to similar emotions or experiences in the minds of the listeners. This view held by Anandavardhana and his followers in the field of literary criticism explains the categorisation of sound into three sectors according to their capability to evoke different emotive experiences.[22]

Sanskrit Literary Theory groups the emotion into three categories according to the feeling-tones, technically known as the 'Gunas'. Such emotions as the Erotic, the Tragic and the Quietistic belong to one category, inasmuch as they melt the mind as soon as they are experienced; this explains the sweetness inherent in them, -- a dose of peculiar flavour, which is inseparable from their texture. Such emotions as the Heroic, the Furious and the Disgustful fall under another category, inasmuch as, when they are experienced the mind glows, giving rise to a burning sensation, that remains inseparably mixed with the peculiar experience springing from enjoyment of these emotions. All emotions again are characterised by perspicuity or lucidity, since experience of all the emotional moods leads to expansion of mind. Placing the different emotional moods under different categories, Sanskrit Literary Theory proceeds to say that while certain groups of letters, categories of compounds and patterns of styles are favourable to evocation of emotive experience belong to one category, other groups of sounds, compounds and styles are favourable to revelation of emotive experience belonging to another category.[23] In case of dramatic composition and dramatic representation the same theory holds good in regard to application of different techniques of acting, known as 'Vrittis' in the terminology of Dramaturgy. All this shows that Sanskrit Literary Theory attaches profound importance to the musical pattern of sound, which bears close linkage to emotion, and consequently the task of evocation of emotive experience. But this does not represent the entire truth and the total position taken by Sanskrit Literary Theory, which attaches equal importance to the explicit sense, and says that the understanding of the explicit always precedes the comprehension of the implicit in Poems.

In its endeavour to explain the relation between the explicit and the implicit, Sanskrit Literary Theory puts forward the parallelism between the meaning of the word and the sentential meaning, and states that, just as the meaning of the word is cognised first and the meaning of the sentence is comprehended next, similarly the explicit meaning is understood first and the comprehension of the implicit follows next. This should not, however, lead the curious reader to think that the understanding of the explicit is a necessary condition for comprehension of the implicit, because even in those cases where the explicit meaning is not understood, the cognition of the implicit takes place. This happens in case of Music, where the musical pattern of sound itself evokes emotive experience in the mind of the listener. In his endeavour to explain the difference between the two cases, -- the case where the musical pattern of the sound alone leads to comprehension of the implicit, and the case where the sound leads first to understanding of the explicit -- Anandavardhana refers to two functions of the word, and says that while in the first case, the word conveys the implicit with the help of its power of suggestion, explicit conjointly raise the implicit into comprehension. In the first case the listener is not required to understand the explicit meaning, because the explicit meaning is not conveyed at all by the musical pattern, which is not, in any way, a significant unit. In the second case the explicit is comprehended first, and the implicit is raised into comprehension at a subsequent stage through the power of signification lying latent in the word and the meaning.[24]

Sanskrit Poetics thus projects the theory in regard to existence of sequence between the comprehension of the conveying agent and the understanding of the implicit, that appears in diverse aspects and the highest form of which is represented by Aesthetic Experience or Rasa. In case of Music, the musical pattern of sound itself independent of the explicit idea gives rise to comprehension of emotive experience: in this case the musical pattern is comprehended first and the exuberance of meaning is experienced next. In the case of a specimen of Poetic Art, the literary symbols are understood first, -- the chain of events and the series of objects, -- the characters and situations, and only after these are recognised, the intended emotive experience is evoked. It becomes incumbent, therefore, to admit the sequence existing between the understanding of the conveying agent, which is represented either by the musical pattern of the sound or by the musical pattern of sound and the pattern of meaning working conjointly, and the implicit idea represented by Aesthetic Experience. Sanskrit Poetics holds the view that, while in some cases the sequence is clearly cognised, in other cases it remains uncomprehended. Taking this principle of classification into account, Sanskrit Literary Theory classifies sublime poetry into two types: the 'Dhvani' of perceptible process and the 'Dhvani' of imperceptible process and in its attempt to link this two-fold classification of 'Dhvani' with the three-fold classification of the symbolic into the symbolic fact, the symbolic figure and the symbolic emotion states that, while the suggested fact and the suggested figure represent 'Dhvani' of perceptible process, the suggested aesthetic experience represents 'Dhvani' of imperceptible process; this, it proclaims, is 'Dhvani' par excellence.[25]

Though Sanskrit Literary Theory puts forward the parallelism of the relation existing between the import of the term and the import of the proposition in its endeavour to explain the relation between the explicit and the implicit, it pronounces a note of caution, and says that the analogy is not to be drawn too far lest it may lead to confusion and complicate the whole issue. The meaning of the word is understood first, no doubt, but once the sentential meaning is comprehended, the meanings of individual words merge themselves completely in the propositional meaning and does not retain their separate existence. The proposition in regard to the understanding of the implicit, however, is different, because after the understanding of the implicit, the explicit does not lose its identity, but continue to retain its existence throughout. It is a fact that the characters and situations, – the chain of events and the series of objects, representing the explicit are located first, and the fantastic emotive experience is comprehended next: the chain of events and the series of objects, however, retain their existence even after evocation of emotive experience. The continuance of 'objective correlative' in the mind of the connoisseur is a pre-condition for experience of emotion, because once they are withdrawn, the emotive experience itself disappears, taking back the refined reader into his original state, when he is bound by considerations of truncated personality. It is not without reason, therefore, that Visvanath describes 'Rasa' or aesthetic experience as a state that lasts as long as the chain of events and series of objects, – the characters and the situations, the 'objective correlatives' in the language of Western Aesthetics retain their existence: when these disappear, emotive experience also disappears. Sanskrit Literary Theory, therefore, states that the parallelism of linkage between the import of the word and the import of the proposition is not applicable in case of linkage between the explicit and the implicit. At best it can be said that, just as the meaning of the word is not traced as something separate from the meaning of the sentence, similarly the explicit is incapable of being traced as something separate from the implicit or so to say, the explicit and the implicit conjointly constitute the content of a single fantastic comprehension, leading to disinterested bliss.[26]

As the parallelism of the relation existing between the cognition of the import of the term and understanding of the import of the proposition is not applicable in case of linkage between the explicit and the implicit, Sanskrit Literary Theory puts forward the parallelism of the relation existing between the jar and the lamp to explain the real position. The lamp reveals the jar, already existing in the dark corner; when the lamp is lit, the jar is revealed, and the lamp also reveals its own self, and the help of any other external factor is not requisitioned to locate the lamp. After the revelation of the jar, the lamp continues to reveal itself and does not withdraw itself from the scene. In explaining the exact relation between the expressed and the unexpressed, Anandavardhana puts forward this parallelism of the 'Lamp and the Jar' and says that just as the lamp continues to reveal itself even after the manifestation of the jar, similarly, the expressed meaning continues to express itself even after the implicit idea is raised into comprehension. The question of withdrawal of the explicit at moments of enjoyment of Poetry does not arise, because, as Sanskrit Literary Theory says, Aesthetic Experience occurs as long as the characters and situations, – the chain of events and the series of objects remain exhibited; when these are withdrawn Aesthetic Experience or 'Rasa' itself disappears.

The parallelism of the relation existing between 'the meaning of the word' and 'the sentential meaning' therefore, is only applicable partially in respect of the relation existing between the explicit and the implicit. This analogy signifies two positive aspects of the linkage between the expressed and the unexpressed. First, the expressed is cognised first and the unexpressed is comprehended next, just as the meaning of the word is understood first and the sentential meaning is grapsed at a subsequent stage. Secondly, once the sentential meaning is cognised, the meanings of individual words do not float in isolation, but rather constitute a single whole: similarly when the implicit is comprehended, the explicit is not traced separately from that and the expressed and the unexpressed conjointly constitute the content of one unified fantastic experience. This helps Anandavardhana to establish his theory that a sequence necessarily exists between the understanding of the explicit and the comprehension of the implicit and to show that the explicit and the implicit constitute the single content of a unified aesthetic experience.

In regard to the nature of the suggestive unit, the stand of Sanskrit Poetics is quite clear. It holds the firm opinion that, the word and the meaning conjointly go to raise into comprehension the symbolic of profound charm. As there is a sequence between the understanding of the word and the comprehension of the meaning, the two do not appear at the same moment, and consequently it is not possible for the two to form a single combination, Sanskrit Theory meets this objection with strong argument, and this argument is furnished by the Philosophy of Sanskrit Grammar, that forms the starting point of the Science of Aesthetics. Philosophy of Sanskrit Grammar considers the form of the word as a fraction of the explicit meaning, and projects the theory that, the knowledge of all meaning is determinant in character, inasmuch as, it is determined by the verbal component. Thus, when the explicit meaning appears, the form of the word also emerges as one of its components, and consequently, nothing prevents the two from forming a single combination. With all emphasis at his command Anandavardhana declares that in the best specimen of Poetic Art, the sound and the explicit idea conjointly raise into comprehension the implicit meaning of inexplicable charm: in such a specimen of literary art the explicit always remains subservient to the implicit in point of strikingness : the music of sound also keeps itself subordinate to the charmingness of the implicit. Sanskrit Literary Theory, thus, expresses the firm opinion that, the credit of raising the symbolic into comprehension does not go either to the music of the sound or to the power of the explicit; it says that to ignore one and to emphasise the other is to project the untruth.[27]

All this indicates the striking similarity between the thought-currents projected by T.S. Eliot and the Sanskrit

Literary Theory, particularly Anandavardhana on a number of issues, namely the issue relating to the factors that are responsible for evocation of emotive experience, the Principle of Propriety, the nature of language to be employed by the literary artists, the multiplicity of the symbolic and the conjoint action of the musical pattern of sound and the musical pattern of meaning. The findings can be summed up in the following paragraphs:

Eliot's concept of 'Objective Correlative' is analogous to the concept of 'Vibhava', 'Anubhava', etc. as contemplated by the Sanskrit Literary Theory. What Sanskrit Literary Theory means by incorporation of the Vibhava, etc. in accordance with the Principle of Propriety, T.S. Eliot means by 'exact equivalence'. When this 'exact equivalence' is not Traced the tragedy does not become successful. The artistic inevitability lies in the complete adequacy of the external factors to the emotion.

T.S. Eliot projects the Theory that Poetry is to retain its linkage with every-day common speech. Sanskrit Literary Theory does not express this view in so many words, possibly, because the position in regard to the language of Sanskrit is different. Sanskrit has got a fixed form of its own, and inspite of the difference in numerous dialects, it has been able to retain its pristine sanctity from the early dawn of human civilization. It is also a fact that Sanskrit is employed in rituals even today and is understood throughout the country. Sanskrit Literary Theory, thus, is not required to state categorically that Poetry should be a return to the common speech, because Sanskrit was the common speech understood by the literate section. But still it feels the necessity of tendering advice to the poets of posterity to make themselves acquainted with the different forms of dialects. It is also obliged to quote a number of stanzas composed in common everyday speech as examples of the grand and sublime Poetry, implying thereby, that it is necessary to know the everyday common language to construct grand and sublime poetry.

Sanskrit Literary Theory repeatedly says that, the expressed is always one, but the unexpressed is characterised by multiplicity. Eliot also says that, the meaning differs from reader to reader, and this meaning may be totally different from the meaning intended to be conveyed by the literary artist. This happens because the meanings pass beyond the frontiers of consciousness of the literary artist.

Neither the aura of sound alone nor the charmingness of meaning alone is responsible for emergence of the implicit. The music of the word and the enchantment of the meaning combine and conjointly raise into comprehension the symbolic. And, as has already been stated, the symbolic par excellence is represented by emotive experience.

This similarity between the thought-currents projected by two systems is so striking that, when one ponders over the areas of similarity, it is likely occur to him that the Indian way of life and thinking had exercised tremendous influence on the mind of T.S. Eliot when he read the Gita and the Upanishads during his studenthood at the University of Cambridge, and many of the Theories projected by Eliot owe their genesis to this influence.

REFERENCES

1. The Use of Poetry and the Use of Criticism : T.S. Eliot, pp. 93-94 (*Selected Prose of T.S. Eliot*, Faber & Faber).
2. Hamlet : T.S. Eliot, p. 48, Ibid.
3. *The Objctive Correlative : Inter-war English Poetry*: M.K. Sen (University of Burdwan, Burdwan).
4. The Evolution of Literature : Mallarme (*Selected Prose, Poems, Essays & Letters*, Tr. by Bradford Cook, p. 132, John Hopkins Press, Baltimore).
5. On this Professor M.K. Sen writes:
   "It is laid down in Hindu Philosophy that huuman nature is made up of three elements, viz. Sattwa, Rajah and Tamah—and, what is more important—human nature is held in perfect balance when these three ingredients are in harmony." —*The Objective Correlative*, p. 41 (University of Burdwan, Burdwan).

6. The Music of Poetry : T.S. Eliot, pp. 110-112 (*Selected Prose of T.S. Eliot*, Faber & Faber, London).
7. *Sāhityadarpaṇa*, III, 15-16.
8. na jāyate tadāsvādo vinā ratyādivāsanām //
   uktaṃ ca Dharmadattena—
   savāsanānāṃ sabhyānāṃ rasasyāsvādanaṃ bhavet /
   nirvāsanāstu raṅgāntaḥ kāṣṭhakuḍyāśmasannibhāḥ //
   — *Sāhityadarpaṇa*, III. 8.
9. *Kāvyaprakāśa*. IV. 27-28.
10. vyāpāro'sti vibhāvādernāmnā sādharaṇīkṛtiḥ //
    and
    parasya na parasyeti mameti na mameti ca /
    tadāsvāde vibhāvādeḥ paricchedo na vidyate //
    —*Sāhityadarpaṇa*, III. 10 & 13.
11. *Dhvanyāloka*, III. 10-14.
    and
    anaucityādṛte nānyad rasabhaṅgasya kāraṇam /
    prasiddhaucityabandhastu rasasyopaniṣat parā //
    kathāśarīramutpādyavastu kāryaṃ tathā tathā /
    yathā rasamayaṃ sarvamevaitat pratibhāsate //
    —Vṛtti on same.
12. *Vākyapadīya*, Brahmakāṇḍa. 44 and 124.
13. santi siddharasaprakhyā ye ca rāmāyaṇādayaḥ /
    kathāśrayā na tairyojyā svecchā rasavirodhinī //
    — *Dhvanyāloka*, Vṛtti on III. 14.
14. The Music of Poetry : T.S. Eliot, pp. 109-112 (*Selected Prose of T.S. Eliot*, Faber & Faber, London)
15. My purpose here is to insist that a 'musical poem' is a poem which has a musical pattern of sound and a musical pattern of the secondary meanings of words which compose it, and that these two patterns are indissoluble and one."
    —The Music of Poetry : T.S. Eliot (*Selected Prose of T.S. Eliot*, Faber & Faber, London), p. 113.
16. "... The ambiguities may be due to the fact that the poem means more, not less, than ordinary speech can communicate." —Ibid., p. 111.
17. The Defence of Shelley and Other Essays : Herbert Read quoting Paul Valery, pp. 159, 162-63 (London).
18. *Kavikaṇṭhābharaṇa* : Kṣemendra,. I (Nirnaya Sagar Edition).
19. Ibid., III.
20. *Dhvanyāloka* : Ānandavardhan, I; Vṛtti on Kārikā 4
    and
    śabdārthaśāsanajñānamātreṇaiva na vedyate /
    vedyate sa tu kāvyārthatattvajñaireva kevalaṃ //
    —*Dhvanyāloka* : Ānandavardhana, I. 7.

21. śabdārthau sahitau vakrakavivyāpāraśālinī /
bandhe vyavasthitau kāvyaṃ tadvidāhlādakāriṇī //
—*Vakroktijīvita*: Kuntakaī, I. 7 (Firma K.L. Mukhopadhyay, Calcutta).

22. *Dhvanyāloka*: Ānandavardhana, I. 13.
23. *Kāvyaprakāśa*: Mammaṭa, VIII. 74-76 (Chowkhamba Sanskrit Samsthan, Varanasi).
24. rasādyanuguṇatvena vyavahāro'rthaśabdayoḥ /
aucityavān yastā etā vṛttayo vividhāḥ smṛtāḥ //
—*Dhvanyāloka,* III. 33 & Vṛtti thereon.
25. *Dhvanyāloka*: Ānandavardhaana, II. 2.
26. yathā hi ghaṭe niṣpanne tadupādānakāraṇānām na pṛthagupālambhastathaiva vākyatadarthe vā pratīteḥ padatadarthānāṃ teṣāṃ tadā vibhaktatayopalambhe vākyārthabuddhireva dūrībhavet. na tveṣa vācyavyaṅ-gyayornyāyaḥ. na hi vyaṅgye pratīyamāne vācyabuddhirdūrībhavati. —*Dhvanyāloka*: Ānandavardhana, III, Vṛtti on 33, p. 236.
27. *Locana*: Abhinavagupta, under Kārikā, I. 13.

CHAPTER IV

Expression and Escape — The Paradox of

Section I

Wordsworth and Eliot

In his preface to the *Lyrical Ballads* Wordsworth describes Poetry as having its origin 'from emotion recollected in tranquility', and asserts that, Poetry is the spontaneous overflow of powerful feelings. In view of Wordsworth when an emotion arises in the mind of the literary artist, his mind gets concentrated on contemplation of this emotion, and the mind gradually attains a state of tranquility, in which all other thoughts are suspended. Wordsworth thinks that a chain of reaction starts the next moment, as a result of which, the tranquility gradually disappears, and the mind gets back its sensitiveness and ability to carve out a new emotion. When tranquility disappears fully, an emotion akin to that, which was the subject of contemplation before appears. It is at this moment that creation of poetry takes place.

In describing the emotion which is produced in the mind of the literary artist after the disappearance of the state of tranquility, Wordsworth asserts that, this is real emotion and actually exists in the mind of the creator. This means that the literary artist actually experiences erotic emotion when he lays his hands upon a specimen of literary art, overflowing with eroticism ; his mind becomes surcharged with real grief and pity when he carves out poetical paintings descriptive of the tragic and so on. The assertion of Wordsworth, thus, admits the real nature of the emotion, experienced by the literary artist at the moment of creation of poetry. Wordsworth thinks that, in this peculiar mental state of the literary artist successful composition generally begins, and throughout the period of this composition, this mood of the artist continues, as a result of which, he does not experience any difficulty in the matter of communication of emotive experience. It is the real emotion of the artist, therefore, which expresses itself in a specimen of Poetic Art, and spontaneously carves out poetic images in its endeavour to express itself.[1]

Wordsworth is aware of the different kinds of emotion, as also its different degrees, but he believes in the principle that, the emotion given expression to by the poet is always qualified by 'various pleasures'. As a result of this, when the emotion is described, the mind of the poet always experiences a sane and wholesome pleasure, or in other words, to quote Wordsworth, the mind remains always "in a state of enjoyment". As the mind of the poet creates a literary composition, it invariably enjoys pleasure; and when the reader concentrates himself on the document of composition produced, his mind also experiences pleasure. It is this pleasure which connects the mind of the creative artist with that of the appreciative reader.

In his endeavour to locate the cause that exists behind the genesis of pleasure in the mind of the reader, Wordsworth arrives at the music or harmonious metrical language; he feels that this music is one of the causes responsible for generation of the complex feelings of delight, and this is the most powerful cause, because it is due to employment of the metrical language that, the effect of poetry is always pleasant and poetry continues to exist as the principal source of gratification of the reader. In this connexion Wordsworth refers to two specimens of compositions on the same subject,

-- one in prose and the other in verse, and says that of the two descriptions, either of passions or manners of characters, each of them equally well-executed, -- the one in prose and the other in verse, -- the verse will be read a hundred times, where the prose will be read only once. This popularity of metrical composition indicates the enchantment of metre and shows that poetry as a whole derives much of its enchantment from the music, -- the harmonious metrical language.[2] This, however, does not mean that the music is the only factor that counts in poetry; matter also is equally important. Wordsworth, therefore, feels that the matter of poetry is to be carefully chosen. He advocates the principle of choosing subjects from common life and employment of ordinary language very close to the real language of men, but at the same time says that, though chosen from common life, the subject should not be contemptible and prosaic. In this connexion Wordsworth quotes two stanzas, -- the first verse from a parody composed by Dr. Johnson and the other from the justly-admired poem "Babes in The Wood". The first specimen runs as follows:

> "I put the hat upon my head
> And walked into the strand,
> And there I met another man
> Whose hat was in his hand."

The justly-admired stanza quoted by Wordsworth is as follows:

> "These pretty Babes with hand in hand
> Went wandering up and down:
> But never more they saw the man
> Approaching from the town."

In both the stanzas the words, and the order of the words differ in no way from the most unimpassioned version. There are such words as 'the hat', 'the strand', 'the hand', 'the town', connected with most familiar ideas; yet the second stanza is admitted as admirable, while the first is a good example of contemptible unsuccessful poetry. Wordsworth believes that this difference in experience of two specimens of poetic Art is due not to any feature of the language employed, but to the nature of the matter itself. While in the second, the matter itself is pretty, in the first it is trifling and consequently uncharming. All this makes the position of Wordsworth clear; while he advocates the theory that subjects of poetry are to be chosen from common life and projects the theory that the endeavour of the literary artists should be to bring language nearer to the real language of men, he feels that the lofty and the charming subjects are to be chosen and that the metrical language is to be preferred to common prose.

Since it is the endeavour of Wordsworth to project a new philosophy of poetry and poetic diction, he takes all care to see that there is not much deviation from tradition and traditional beliefs and standards, endeared so long by the reader. He knows that the reader likes pleasure and reads poetry for the sake of attainment of delight, but at the same time, the truth of the fact is that, the reader is not only keen to be pleased, but to be pleased in that particular way in which he has been accustomed to be pleased. This anxiety to conceive of such a poetry that can please the reader in the particular way in which he has been accustomed to be pleased has prevented Wordsworth from projecting a more bold theory of poetry, that can present a glimpse of the Infinite. It is not that Wordsworth is not aware of the inexhaustible power of language : on the other hand, he is very much conscious of this indefinite power, and knows that it is possible for poetry to give other enjoyment, – of a purer, more lasting and more exquisite nature, – that it is possible for the poetry to interest mankind permanently by the multiplicity of its meanings and quality of moral relations. But the restraint imposed by considerations of the set beliefs of the reader prompts him to declare that the power of any art is limited. In the view of Wordsworth, thus, the literary artist gives expression to the emotion, which is very much real, lying latent in him, that this emotion expressed in poetical painting is necessarily mixed with pleasure, – that when the passions and emotions are transferred to the reader, pleasure also is transmitted to him, – that the harmonious metrical language and the charmingness of matter both are responsible for enchantment of poetry, and, – that though the powers of languages are not limited, the power of art is limited to a great extent.[3]

In his critical Essay entitled *Tradition and the Individual Talent* T.S. Eliot controverts the theory proposed by William Wordsworth, – the theory that poetry owes its genesis to "emotion recollected in tranquility" and that the emotion is the actual emotion experienced by the poet at the time of carving out poetical paintings. Eliot propounds the theory of 'Impersonality' in Art and says that the emotions that are given expression to through the medium of poetry do not represent the actual emotions experienced by the poet, but rather the transmuted feelings of the literary artist. The poet definitely experiences certain feelings before composition of poetry, – emotions that may be provoked by particular event of his life, but these personal emotions are not given expression to through the medium of poetry. Eliot extends recognition to the process of transmutation, and says that the ordinary experiences generated in the mind of the literary artist are soon transmuted into extra-ordinary and generalised ones, as a result of which a distinction appears between 'the mind which experiences' and 'the mind which creates'. It is because of this process of metamorphosis of the ordinary into the extra-ordinary, – of the particular into universal, of the personal into the impersonal, that it becomes possible for the general reader to experience his passions and actions in the passions and actions presented in poetry, and identify himself easily with characters and situations depicted therein.

Eliot, thus, draws the line of demarcation between the Poet, the man, and the Poet, the literary artist, and says that the emotions presented by the literary artist are not the particular and personal emotions experienced by the poet in his individual capacity. The particular emotions of the individual poet are simple and crude : the emotion presented in poetry, however, is a complex one, being an amalgam of diverse experiences. In this connection, Eliot pronounces a note of caution to literary artists of posterity by declaring that it is not proper for the artists to seek for unusual or new human emotions, because such unusual emotions and new human relations presented in poetry convert the specimen of literary art into a close-door room, making impossible the access of connoisseurs to it. In fact, Eliot describes the tendency to seek for new human emotions to express them in poetry as eccentricity in poetry, because, as he says, the search for novelty is likely to end in discovery of the trifling and the stale.

Eliot, thus, gives expression to his belief that the poet is to deal with the permanent moods, that are experienced by men, and that are incapable of being eradicated from the mental plane being common characteristic feature of all members of humanity. In his individual capacity, the poet experiences these emotions in their raw forms, but soon they are transmuted to subtler forms, where brute elements disappear and what remain are the transformed mature emotions arrived at through extensive cultural exercise. The 'raw' emotion belongs to the individual poet, while the sublimated emotion belongs to the artist engaged in the process of creation. It is this sublimated emotion that connects the literary artist with the literary artist, — the literary artist with the reader, and the reader with the reader.[4]

In view of T.S. Eliot, therefore, the business of the poet is not to find new emotions or new human relations, but to use the ordinary and familiar ones, that are experienced normally by all members of humanity, and in working them up in Poetry to express feelings, which may not have been experienced by him at all. The literary artist is not in a position to do this job with emotions that are familiar to him, he is to take the help of emotions that have been experienced by him, as also those that have never been experienced by him. Since a line of demarcation exists between the 'mind which experiences' and the 'mind which creates', there is definitely a distinction between the actual emotions experienced by the poet in his individual capacity and the sublimated emotion given expression to by him in his capacity as the literary artist. The reason is obvious. A specimen of poetic art presenting the personal feeling of the poet may not generate any interest in the mind of the connoisseur who may search for his own personal feelings in vain in those presented in poetry. When the personal emotions attain an impersonal form and the particular becomes generalised, it becomes possible for the connoisseur to trace his own feelings in those depicated in the specimen of poetic art and to satisfy his craving to find out his relation with all members of humanity. All these considerations prompt Eliot to declare the formula suggested by Wordsworth, – the formula that 'Poetry takes its origin in emotions recollected in tranquillity' as an inexact formula and to refute his theory that, the emotion 'does actually exist in the mind' of the creative artist. The emotion given expression to in the poem in neither emotion nor is it a case of recollection. And this is so, because recollection can be predicated only of that entity in regard to which experience have been derived earlier; the emotion presented in poetry is not real and may not have been experienced at all by the poet in his individual capacity. Consequently, the proposition in regard to recollection of the emotion is a myth. The emotion that is given expression to by 'the mind which creates' is neither actual, nor does its recollection take place in any way.

Continuing his cricism of Wordsworth's formula of 'emotion recollected in tranquility', Eliot says that this state of tranquility is incapable of being asserted in the description of the poetic process, because in the writing of poetry, there has necessarily to be some conscious and deliberate attempt in the matter of selection of expressions and conception of plots. Eliot endorses the proposition of concentration, projected by Wordsworth, but says that this is not ordinary concentration, inasmuch as, a new thing results from this concentration, and this new thing is nothing other than the transmuted universal emotion. Concentration which gives birth to a new entity cannot be described as concentration on the personal emotion of the poet, because such concentration cannot generate any new thing or new experience and consequently, the state of mind in which the mind searches after appropriate plots and incidents, idioms and expressions, metres and figures cannot be regarded as a complete state of 'tranquility'. The declaration of Eliot, therefore, is that, the emotion given expression to in poetry is not the actual emotion experienced by the poet; its recollection does not take place; and that no state of tranquility is produced in the mind of the literary artist at the time of carving out of poetical paintings.

In the view of T.S. Eliot, while concentration and contemplation are essential requirements for genesis of poetry, there is necessity of some amount of conscious effort for carving out poetical paintings, because an artistic finish cannot be given to poetry unless the help of intellectual power is requisitioned. Eliot, therefore, extends recognition to both the unconscious process of concentration and the conscious process of application of creative faculty for creation of the document of literary art. There may be moments of 'tranquility' when the mind of the literary artist rests on the delight of experiencing the emotion, but there are moments also when he is required to apply his mind consciously to the art of production of literary symbols and giving a finished form to them, - a form through which they can be in a position to transplant the emotion experienced in the mind of the reader. The process of creation of poetry, therefore, is both unconscious and conscious.

At this moment of time Eliot pronounces a note of caution by saying that the poet is required to take recourse to these two processes at appropriate times, because even a small errors in the point of selection of appropriate time is likely to vitiate the entire art by making the specimen of poetry 'personal' in character. While a successful literary artist knows where to remain unconscious and where to become conscious, an unsuccessful one remains unconscious, where 'he ought to be conscious' and 'conscious' where 'he ought to be unconscious'. And both these errors make literary artists 'personal'. The transmutation of the ordinary raw emotion into the sublimated emotion takes place unconsciously in the mind of the artist. If the poet remains extremely conscious at this material point of time and takes care to see that the raw emotion remains as it is, then the poetry is sure to fail, because it is the sublimated emotion only that can be experienced by all like-minded persons. In a similar manner at the time of selecting the appropriate poetic tissue and creation of the significant literary symbol, the poet is required to apply a conscious effort, inasmuch as, intellect has a great role to play in the matter of giving a finished form to the literary symbol. If the poet remains unconscious at this material point of time and does not apply his intellect properly in building up the poetic texture, the symbol so created is likely to prove itself a weak one, not competent to raise into comprehension the emotive experience, desired to be transplanted in the mind of the reader. Eliot, therefore, is perfectly right when he says that, the tendency of becoming conscious where he should be unconscious and that of remaining unconscious, where he should be conscious, both these tend to make the poet personal and make the specimen of literary art also an unsuccessful one. And this is so, because the ideal of 'Impersonality in Poetry' is the only ideal that is to be translated into action.[5]

A comparative estimate of the view-points of William Wordsworth and T.S. Eliot thus indicates the following points:

(1) While Wordsworth thinks that Poetry has its genesis in emotion recollected in tranquility, Eliot believes that this is an inexact formula, because neither recollection takes place nor is a situation of tranquility produced.

(2) While Wordsworth projects the theory that the emotion generated in the mind of the literary artist is the real emotion, T.S. Eliot believes that this is not the personal emotion of the poet. The process of creation of poetry, as Eliot points out, is a continuous process of self-denial. Poetry, thus, is not an expression of personality: it is an escape from personality. This statement may appear to be paradoxical, but what Eliot means is that, poetry does not give expression to the poet's personal emotion in Poetry, but rather to the universal emotion: similarly, the poet does not give expression to the narrow individual mood, but to the generalised feeling that can be shared by all members of humanity. All these mean that, the ego-boundaries of the creative artist expand at the time of concentration on the emotive experience and creation of literary symbols, competent to raise the unique experience into comprehension. This does not mean that personality has no role to play in production of poetry. As a matter of fact, poetry cannot be produced unless the artist remains conscious of his self. What is meant is this that, his small ego is to be put into slumber and wider ego nourished and nurtured so that, he can trace his own experience in the experience of humanity and the experience of the wider community in that of his own self. Eliot is fully aware of this distinction between 'small ego' and 'wider ego' to signify which the expression 'individuality' and 'personality' respectively had been employed by Tagore. Giving expression to this awareness of distinction between 'narrow individuality' and 'bigger personality', Eliot rightly remarks: "but, of course, only whose who have personality and emotions know what it means to want to escape from these things."

Section II

Indian Theory of Escape

Sanskrit Poetics considers 'Rasa' as the be-all and end-all of all poetry, and declares in unequivocal terms the truth that the prime purpose of poetry is to evoke an emotive experience in the mind of the connoisseur, -- to transplant the universal experience generated in the mind of the literary artist to the mind of the refined reader, so that the literary artist and the connoisseur can share the experience together. It is not without reason, therefore, that Sanskrit Literary Theory considers the artist and the connoisseur as the two parts essential for successful completion of the process of transplantation, representing the poetic circuit. The effort of the artist to give vent to his experience becomes successful only when it is caught by the appreciator or, in other words, it becomes able to evoke a corresponding experience in the mind of the appreciator. Similarly, the desire of the appreciative reader to expand his ego-boundaries is brought into consummation only when he gets an opportunity of making himself absorbed on the generalised experience presented by the literary artist. In the absence of the literary artist the desire of the appreciator to have a taste of his emotive experience in a wider perspective remains unfructified: in a similar manner, in the absence of the appreciative reader, the desire of the artist to give expression to the transmuted emotion remains unfulfilled. There is sufficient justification therefore in the claim put forward by Sanskrit Literary Theory that the artist and the appreciator conjointly constitute the essence of Poetic Art.[6]

Sanskrit Poetics discusses 'Rasa' mainly in the context of the refined appreciator, and describes him as constituting the locus of 'Rasa'. It goes on to say that 'Rasa' belongs neither to the original personage nor to the work of Poetic Art, but to the refined appreciator, who savours the delight of emotive experience at the time of appreciation of poetry. Sanskrit Theory attaches greater importance to the refined reader, who is known as the 'Sahridaya' in the terminology of Indian Theory. The 'Sahridaya' is a man of refined aesthetic instinct; he has made himself acquainted with the creation of master artists, and consequently his mind has become full of responsiveness to the events and characters, situations and chains of events, presented in the document of literary art. Such a refined reader, – a sensitive appreciator is a man of trained intellectual powers, as a result of the training obtained by whom it becomes easy for him to share the generalised experience of the poet and escape from the boundaries of truncated ego in the manner the poet escapes.

Due to the great emphasis placed by Sanskrit Literary Theory on the connoisseur, a wrong notion has developed in some quarters that Sanskrit Poetics does not consider the literary artist as the experiencer of 'Rasa'. This, however, is a wrong notion, because Abhinavagupta, following Anandavardhana has made it abundantly clear that 'Rasa' belongs as much to the literary artist as to the responsive reader. How can the literary artist, who extends an opportunity to the refined appreciator to savour the delight of 'Rasa', himself remain dry and inexperienced to the delight of the fantastic emotion created by literary art? Unless the literary artist himself experiences generalised emotion, it becomes impossible for him to transplant the peculiar experience into the mind of the connoisseur. In describing the role of poetic intuition, Abhinavagupta therefore, says that, poetic faculty consists in the power to carve out a poetical painting, constituting the symbol of the experience of the artist, when his mind becomes over-flooded with 'Rasa' or the universalised impersonal experience. This means that in the view of Abhinavagupta also Rasa belongs as much to the artist as to the connoisseur. In describing the creative process Anandavardhana states that, as the mind of the artist gets absorbed in contemplation of the emotional mood, the poetical painting automatically rushes forth from the fountainhead of his poetic imagination, as a result of which the texture of poetry proves itself to be a spontaneous one. In describing autonomy of poetry, Anandavardhana again points out that, when the mind of the literary artist becomes surcharged with sweet emotion, what is produced becomes soft and sweet and is savoured with delight by all connoisseurs; on the other hand, when the literary artist fails to get his mind absorbed in a generalised emotive experience, what is produced turns to be dry. In explaining this general proposition, thrown by Anandavardhana, Abhinavagupta states that, what is acatually meant is that, in case of a really enchanting specimen of poetic art the literary artist is able to effect transmutation of his personal experience and to give expression to the impersonalized universal experience: in case of a specimen of poetic art which falls flat on the appreciator, on the other hand, the artist is unable to effect metamorphosis of his personal experience. In case of the former, the artist transcends the boundaries of truncated ego : in case of the latter, the artist moves within the narrow limits imposed by his small ego. In case of enchanting documents of literary art, therefore, there is escape, while in case of disenchanting specimens of poetic art, there is expression of small personality. Sanskrit Literary Art, therefore, takes note of this distinction between 'expression' and 'escape' and declares in unequivocal terms the Theory that, it is 'escape from personality' which makes poetry good and sublime.[7]

It is necessary at this material point of time to introduce the concept of 'Rasa', which is so familiar in Sanskrit Literary Theory. The small aphorism of Bharata, which states that the 'Rasa' is produced through conjunction of the excitant, the ensuent and the accessories with the 'permanent mood' forms the starting point of all discussions on 'Rasa'. Different interpretations of this terse aphorism give rise to different doctrines on Aesthetic Realisation. While earlier doctrines ignore the literary art altogether, later theories put equal emphasis on the artist and the connoisseur, and when Abhinavagupta appears in the field with his profound interpretation of the aphorism, he points out to both the artist and the appreciator as constituting the locus of 'Rasa', and goes so far as to declare the two as completing the circuit of Poetic Art.

Bhattalollata is the first commentator to expound the theory of Aesthetic Experience, propounded by Bharata. Since the chief intention of Bharata was to explain Aesthetic Experience in the context of drama, Bhattalollata has explained the principle in the context of drama, and in doing this he has kept in mind the refined spectator to whom alone the specimen of dramatic art appeals. Bhattalollata has preferred to accept the principle of profound strength of perception and consequently, to assert that the refined spectator derives refined and sane pleasure from perceptive knowledge of emotive experience generated in the original character, taken as identical with the actor. The steps in Bhattalollata's theory of Aesthetic Experience are as follows:

(a) The refined spectator sees the actor before him. As long as the enactment of the drama continues, he takes the actor as identical with the dramatic personae. This knowledge in regard to identity of the actors with the original characters is an erroneous knowledge.

(b) At a subsequent stage the spectator perceives the emotive experience generated in the mind of the original character, now taken as identical with the actor.

(c) In the perceptive knowledge thus derived there are two portions — the first being "this particular actor 'X' is identical with the particular character 'Y'" and the second being "'Y' is possessed of emotive experience".

(d) In explaining generation of perceptive knowledge in regard to both these fractions constituting the content of comprehension, Lollata states that, while the first fragment is coginsed through ordinary perception, the second fragment is made known through extra-ordinary perception.[8]

Thus, Lollata explains 'Rasa' in regard to the refined spectator alone, and he ignores completely the dramatist and the actor. In explaining the background training of the refined spectator, Visvanatha says that, only those who are endowed with appreciative genius are in a position to experience 'Rasa' : persons who are devoid of this appreciative faculty are comparable to the pillars of the auditorium, that does not derive any emotive experience whatsoever from presentation of drama. It is curious that, Bharata also explains 'Rasa' in regard to the refined appreciator alone, and ignores completely the literary artist, who lies behind the generation of the whole technique of presentation of aesthetic experience. This great lacuna inherent in the doctrine of Aesthetic Realisation, propounded by Bharata is taken note of by Bhattanayaka and Abhinavagupta, who assert that 'Rasa' does not belong to the connoisseur alone; but it belongs as much to the artist as to the connoisseur, because unless the artist himself experiences and elevates the brute personal emotion into fantastic universalised emotion, he cannot transplant it in the mind of the appreciative enjoyer. After all, the Art of Poetry consists in the art of transplantation of universalised experience from one mind to another, and until generalisation of the experience takes place in the mind of the artist, it cannot be transplanted to the appreciator. It is extremely significant, therefore, that Bhattanayaka describes the hero, the literary artist and the refined reader as sharing the common experience and declares that, the essence of aesthetic realisation rests in sharability of experience. But before this doctrine of Bhattanayaka sets at rest other theories, a number of theories emerged, each trying to explain the process of Aesthetic Experience in their own way, but none of them making any significant contribution in the area. Of these minor theories, however, the doctrine propounded by Srisankuka deserves mention because of certain new flashes of ideas, – flashes that have been incorporated by Abhinavagupta in his great theory.

Sankuka advances a Theory, which bears close parallelism to that projected by Lollata. This theory also explains 'Rasa' in the context of drama, and ignores completely the specimen of poetic art as also the literary artist, who is behind the creation of the particular drama. Like Lollata, Sankuka also asserts that, during the total period of dramatic representation the spectator is persuaded to believe that the actor is identical with the original character. Agreeing with Lollata, he also says that knowledge of emotive experience belonging to the original character now taken as identical with the actor causes sane and wholesome pleasure in the mind of the spectator. There is, however, difference between the theories adumbrated by these two theoreticians in respect of the nature of knowledge derived in regard to both the identity of the character with the actor and his emotive experience.

While Lollata thinks that the knowledge which the spectator has in regard to the identity of the actor with the character is an eroneous knowledge, Sankuka affirms that this is a peculiar type of knowledge, different from right or wrong notion and at the same time from doubtful or similar cognition. It does not belong to the category of right notion, inasmuch as, the spectator does not have this knowledge as "the actor X is identical with the character Y" and "the character Y is identical with actor X". Nor does he derives at the first instance such knowledge as, "the actor X is identical with the character Y" and this knowledge is removed by a later knowledge as "this actor X is different from the character Y". Continuing his argument, Sankuka states that at time of witnessing a dramatic representation, the spectator does not have this notion that "the actor X may or may not be identical with the character Y"; nor does he become a victim to such a notion that the "actor X is similar to the character Y". In view of the fact that the knowledge which the spectator has in regard to the original character is a knowledge completely different from the four recognised types of cognition, Sankuka floats the postulation of a new type of knowledge, – the knowledge which one has of the horse in regard to the picture of the horse. The picture of the horse is neither identical with the horse nor is it different from it; nor does the experiencer has any doubt as to whether this is the horse or not; nor does he take the picture of the horse as one resembling the horse. The philosophy behind postulation of this new category of knowledge is that the experience which the spectator derives at the time of witnessing a specimen of dramatic art is a peculiar one and is not capable of being identified with any type of notion experienced in the ordinary world. This postulation of a new category of experience leads a new colour to the Theory propounded by Sankuka, and extends an opportunity to Abhinavagupta to build up his great theory by utilising this postulation.

In regard to the knowledge concerning the emotive experience, Sankuka differs from Lollata and postulates the theory of inferential knowledge. While Lollata expresses the opinion that, the refined spectator derives perceptive knowledge of the emotion belonging to the character, now taken as identical with the character, Sankuka favours the view that the emotive experience of the original character is comprehended through the process of inference. Later expounders of the theory propounded by Sankuka take great pains in establishing the strength of inference in case of conflict between perception and inference in a number of situations and show that 'in the situation presented in witnessing of a theatrical performance, the strength of the process of inference is to be admitted over that of perception.

The steps, therefore, in Sankuka's theory of Aesthetic Experience are as follows:

(a)The refined spectator takes the actor as identical with the character, and this notion continues throughout the period of dramatic representation;

(b)The knowledge which the spectator has of the character in regard to the actor is a different type of knowledge, capable of being described as analogous to the knowledge which one has of the horse in respect of the picture of the horse;

(c)The emotive experience generated in the mind of the character, now taken as identical with the actor is comprehended by the spectator through the process of Inference;

(d)This knowledge of the emotion belonging to the original character causes sane and wholesome pleasure in the mind of the refined spectator.[9]

Sankuka, thus, explains 'Rasa' in the context of dramatic representation, and points out to the refined spectator as constituting the locus of 'Rasa'. The weakness of this theory lies in the fact that, it does not discuss as to how inference of an emotion belonging to one can generate bliss in the mind of another nor does it describe 'Rasa' in regard to the dramatist, who is mainly responsible for presenting the characters and situations, chains of events and series of objects competent to arouse emotive experience in the mind of the spectator. It is because of this serious lacuna that the theory is rejected by later theoreticians, who try to go deep into the problem of attainment of Aesthetic Experience. These theoreticians, particularly Bhattanayaka and Abhinavagupta structure their own theories at a subsequent period, -- theories in which 'Rasa' is described both in the context of the artist and the appreciator and the process of transmutation of emotion finds its due recognition.

Coming to Bhattanayaka one finds the emphasis shifted from the external factors to the internal experience of the connoisseur, who is accepted as a man of trained intellectual powers. Bhattanayaka refuses to accept the proposition that, the perceptive or inferential knowledge of an emotive experience belonging to one is in a position to cause extra-normal pleasure in the mind of another and consequently he tries to explain the whole process of aesthetic realisation in a different manner. In his endeavour to achieve this end, Bhattanayaka is constrained to take the n functions, -- the function leading to generalisation and the function leading to steadiness of the mind. These two new functions, technically known as 'Bhavakatva' and 'Bhojakatva' receive recognition for the first time at the hands of Bhattanayaka and the contribution made by this literary theoretician to the field of literary criticism, therefore, is extremely significant.

In the theory propounded by Bhattanayaka, the refined appreciator acquires prominence, and it is mainly in the context of the connoisseur that 'Rasa' is admitted to be explained. At the time of appreciation of poetry the connoisseur first of all makes himself acquainted with the characters and situations, chain of events and series of objects, and these are made known through the ordinary function of denotation pertaining to words. After this, the function of 'Bhavakatva' starts operating as a result of which the characters and situations and chain of events and series of objects are comprehended in their universal aspect, that is to say, as divested of all particularities. This means that the character 'X' bearing a particular relationship to the character 'Y' does not appear in this form to the connoisseur, who recognises 'X' as the universal man and 'Y' also as the generalised lady. But this represents only one aspect of the process of generalisation. There is another deeper aspect of this process, and in this profoundly significant aspect, the process of universalization takes place in the internal mind of the appreciator. This means that at the time of appreciation of a specimen of literary art, the refined reader transcends the boundary imposed by small ego, and, for the time being at least, considers himself to be one with the general community of persons of trained intellectual powers. This 'escape' of the refined reader from the prison of truncated ego, Bhattanayaka asserts, constitutes the essential pre-condition necessary for attainment of aesthetic experience.

When this miracle of 'escape' occurs and the emotive experience, aroused in the mind of the connoisseur is generalised and constitutes the chief content of contemplation, the mind of the appreciator becomes steady and free from oscillation. Attainment of delight springs from this steadiness of the mind, since, according to Indian Theory, all happiness springs from the steadiness of the mind and all misery flows from its oscillation. Genesis of steadiness, Bhattanayaka asserts, is effected by the function of 'Bhojakatva' which is in a position to create miracles by changing completely the psychology of the comprehender.

In the view of Bhattanayaka, thus, the following steps are traceable in the process of attainment of Aesthetic Experience:

(a)The appreciator first of all makes himself acquainted with the characters and situations, chains of events and series of objects. This acquaintance is effected through the ordinary function of denotation.

(b)As soon as this takes place, the new function of Bhattanayaka known as Bhavakatva which belongs to poetic expression alone starts operating in two planes.

(c)Operating at the external level, the function of Bhavakatva presents the characters and circumstances, events and objects in their generalised forms: operating in the internal area it effects 'escape' of the comprehender from the bondage of 'small ego', as a result of which he considers himself to be one with the community of the connoisseurs.

(d)When all this takes place, the mind of the comprehender becomes steady and free from all oscillations. This is the result of the operation of the process of Bhojakatva.

(e)When all this happens, the mind of the comprehender naturally experiences sane and wholesome pleasure.[10]

Though Bhattanayaka mainly explains 'Rasa' in the context of the connoisseur, he employs certain terms which shows that he is aware of the intricacies of poetic process and is conscious of the fact that 'Rasa' is experienced equally by the literary artist. In citing the salient features of the doctrine propounded by Bhattanayaka, later commentators say that, according to this learned critic, the emotive experience of the hero, the literary artist and the refined reader meet on a common platform. The emotive experience of the literary artist and the sensitive comprehender cannot meet on a common platform unless both rise above the boundaries of small individual planes and place themselves on a bigger footing. The experience of the literary artist is peculiar to the poet: this cannot be shared by the refined reader unless it is universalised. Bhattanayaka realises this truth lying behind the production as well as appreciation of poetry, and maintains that greatness of a specimen of literary art depends on its ability in transplanting the emotive experience of the literary artist in the mind of the sensitive reader. This transplantation becomes possible only because the creative artist shakes off his narrow individuality and gives expression to feelings, that are common to all members of humanity. A literary artist who keeps himself confined within the boundaries of 'small ego' carves out private images; an artist who escapes from this, on the other hand, creates bold images, that constitute the common meeting ground of the minds of humanity at large. Bhattanayaka, thus, accepts the proposition of 'escape' and awareness of the literary artist in regard to his bigger personality, but he does not proceed to elaborate it.

Rasa in the context of the literary artist finds fuller exposition at the hands of Abhinavagupta who, following his great master, Anandavardhana, expresses the opinion that 'Rasa' is experienced as much by the literary artist as by the refined appreciator. Explaining the aphorism of Bharata, Abhinavagupta says that, the function of suggestion plays a significant role in the matter of attainment of aesthetic experience, and at the time of appreciation of poetry, what is experienced is the bliss associated with the bigger self of the experiencer, and not the emotive experience belonging to the original character or the trained actor.

Abhinavagupta expounds the theory that at the time of appreciation of poetry the refined reader, first of all, makes himself acquainted with the characters and situations, the chains of events and series of objects and thereafter locates the emotive experience belonging to the original character. As soon as this location takes place, the permanent mood lying latent in the mind of the appreciator is called into play, as a result of which a similar emotive experience occurs in him. When the mind of the appreciator gets itself concentrated on this emotive experience, it loses its individual traits and appears as the emotive experience of humanity at large. When this concentration and appearance of emotive experience in its universal aspect takes place, the mind of the appreciator naturally savours sane and wholesome delight, springing from repose of the bigger self on itself.

Later theoreticians, while commenting on the theory adumbrated by Abhinavagupta, maintain that at the time of attainment of emotive experience the function of suggestion removes the veil of ignorance covering the bliss portion of the self as a result of which the bliss associated with the self of the comprehender shines in its full glory. 'Rasa' therefore, is not something external to the comprehender; it consists in savouring of the self by the self itself and experience of sane and whole-some pleasure, arising out of this splendid process of savouring.

The steps necessary for attainment of aesthetic experience in the theory of Abhinavagupta, therefore, are as follows:

(a)The refined appreciator first of all makes himself acquainted with the characters and situations, chains of events and series of objects represented in the document of literary art and ascertains the permanent mood belonging to the original characater.

(b)Thereafter, the corresponding permanent mood lying latent in the refined appreciator is called into play, as a result of which he experiences a corresponding emotion in his mind.

(c)This emotive experience is subsequently universalised, as a result of which the appreciator becomes able to trace the experience of humanity in his experience and his emotive experince in the emotive experience of the humanity at large.

(d)The mind of the appreciator makes itself free from limitations imposed by small ego, and gets itself concentrated on the universalised emotive experience.

(e)When this happens, the bigger self of the apprehender expresses itself in its full glory and as 'bliss' constitutes a part and parcel of the self, this is experienced in natural course.

(f) 'Rasa', therefore, consists in experience of bliss associated with one's own self by his own self.[11]

Abhinavagupta expresses in unequivocal terms the opinion that, 'Rasa' is experienced by the literary artist as well, and that all the steps indicated above take place in the mind of the literary artist endowed with creative genius at the time of creation of poetry. Poetry, after all, is an expression of emotion, but neither this expression is an ordinary process of putting a phraseology nor is this emotion an ordinary emotion belonging to the personal life of the poet. This emotion is a transmuted form of the ordinary emotion, or in other words, it is a universalised emotion, which is capable of being experienced by all members of humanity. Abhinavagupta realises the difficulty associated with expression of personal emotions, because this expression of emotion, which is purely personal to the literary artist is likely to create a 'private image', -- a 'closed symbol', incapable of being deciphered by the sensitive reader. It is for this reason that, he projects the theory of 'escape from the shackless of truncated ego', -- an escape which is necessary for universalisation of the artist and his pleasurable rest in the bigger self. When the pulls and pressures of small ego are sent to the background, the expanded ego shines in its full glory. The emotion, that is savoured by this expanded ego, may be artificial as far as the personal life of the literary artist is concerned. But this is really emotive experience from the point of view of art, inasmuch as, it enables the artist to create a poetical painting, that can provide a common meeting ground to all sensitive readers. Abhinavagupta, therefore, explains creative faculty as the power of carving out a clear poetical painting by a literary artist, whose mind experiences an afflux of universalised emotion. Unless this generalised emotion is experienced by the literary artist, it does not become possible for him to carve out general poetical paintings, -- real art symbols of emotive experience.

It is interesting to note that Anandavardhana, the great

master of Abhinavagupta, also admits this principle. He also describes the literary artist as savouring the delight of 'Rasa' at the time of creation of poetry. In describing the principle of autonomy in poetry, Anandavardhana states that 'the literary artist is supreme in his own sphere, and that, the entire creation takes different forms accordng to his mental inclination. If the artist is suffused with emotional mood the universe takes a delightful and brilliant form: if, on the other hand, he is not responsive to the softer sentiments, the whole creation appears as dry and tasteless'. This concept of 'Autonomy in Poetry' itself, floated by Anandavardhana shows that he does not believe in the principle of expression of personal emotion by the literary artist. What he intends to project is that, the emotion presented in poetry is universal: it may not have any place in the personal life of the poet.[12]

That Anandavardhana is conscious of the fact that, the literary artist constitutes as much the locus of 'Rasa' as the refined appreciator is evident from his statement in regard to the character of the poetic creation as also the principle relating to employment of poetic figures in poetry. In describing the genesis of the first specimen of poetic art, Anandavardhana says that the Ramayana, which represents the first document of literary art is nothing but an outward expression of the tragic emotion, generated in the mind of the literary artist. Anandavardhana himself draws the line of distinction between the 'brute' emotion which belongs to the bird and 'transmuted' emotion which belongs to the literary artist, and explains that, when an ordinary emotion is converted into sublimated universal emotion in the mind of the literary artist, it overflows his mental apparatus and while coming out in the external world assumes the form of the Ramayana.

In expounding the principle relating to employment of poetic figures in the poetry, Anandavardhana says that as the mind of the poet remains absorbed on 'Rasa', generated in his mind, the poetic figures rush forth spontaneously from his imagination, as a result of which he is not required to take recourse to any laborious search for improvisation of poetic figures. The ideal poetic figure, as visualised by Anandavardhana, thus, is that, which is brought into being by 'Rasa' generated in the mind of the literary artist in its endeavour to give expression to its own self. This 'expression' contemplated in the poetic process is not expression of personal emotion, that lives in the personal life of the poet, – but rather of sublimated universal emotion, that resides in the art alone. This distinction which Anandavardhana makes between the real emotion residing in the personal life of the literary artist and sublimated idealised emotion residing in art is to be taken note of, while making an assessment of the contribution of Sanskrit Literary Theory to the problems of 'expression' and 'escape'.

It is curious to note that Anandavardhana describes the whole document of literary art also as possessed of 'Rasa', giving thereby a wider field to the concept. In several places Anandavardhana emphasises the necessity of presenting the sublimated idealised emotive experience in the specimen of literary art, and says that, the very fact that, a poem does not present this experience testifies to the weak imagination of the literary artist: consequently, such a document of literary art can never attain the height of the sublime poetry. In the theory of Anandavardhana, thus, Rasa belongs to the appreciative connoisseur, – the literary artist of strong creative faculty, – and the document of literary art as a whole, that represents a specimen of grand and sublimated poetry. Consequently it is not wrong to deduce the conclusion that Anandavardhana gives a wider spectrum to the concept of 'Rasa' and accepts the principle that, the emotive experience signified by the expression 'Rasa' belongs as much to the literary artist as to the refined reader and the sublime poetry. Abhinavagupta explains this point further and expounds the theory that, the literary artist in the process of carving out poetical paintings gives expression to the generalised emotion that exists in the realm of art alone. This virtually is a re-statement of the doctrine of 'Autonomy in Poetry' projected so faithfully by Anandavardhana.

Section III

Synthesis

The theory in regard to creation and appreciation of poetry, as propounded by T.S. Eliot bears amazing similarity with the doctrines adumbrated by Indian Literary Criticism on the same issue. Both T.S. Eliot and Indian Literary Theoreticians observe that poetry is at the same time an 'expression' of emotion and an 'escape' from it: both emphatically observe that the emotion expressed in poetry does not live in the personal life of the creative artist, but that it lives in the realm of 'Art' and 'Art' alone; both, in the similar manner, assert that the literary artist is to use the ordinary emotions, but he is required to give a new shape to them at the time of carving out poetical paintings. Finally, both observe that there may be some element of passive attending upon the event, intended to be delineated in the specimen of poetic art, but there is a great deal in the writing of poetry which has got to be conscious and deliberate. The Indian viewpoints which get a beautiful exposition at the hands of Anandavardhana and Abhinavagupta, receive a clear treatment at the hands of neo-rhetoricians, the viewpoints of whom are cited by Jagannatha. The neo-rhetorician does not extend recognition to the new functions, acknowledged in the scheme of earlier theoreticians, but asserts that due to a defect, the literary artist and the appreciative reader think that he is identical with the original personage, and when this sense dawns, bliss is savoured by them in natural course. The defect contemplated in this system owes its genesis to 'passive attending' upon the event; it makes the literary artist, as well as the appreciative reader feel that he is identical with the original character. Since this sense of identity cannot take place unless the personal emotions of the artist and the reader are raised to a universal status and the experience of the original character is also elevated to an impersonal status, it is to be admitted that the transformation of personal into the impersonal takes place in all the spheres both at the time of creation of poetry as also at the time of its appreciation. In his endeavour to explain as to why in such a situation the literary artist is prompted to create a document of literary art presenting the 'Tragic' or the appreciator feels attracted to it, the neo-rhetoricians put forward a number of views, some of which states that though the real tragic may originate pain and anguish, the imaginary is not in a position to do so, and some assert that, the experience of the tragic is incapable of producing unmixed bliss: what is given rise to is rather painful pleasure or pleasurable pain. In conclusion, the neo-rhetorician says that the entire process of metamorphosis of the personal into impersonal and the savour of unmixed bliss even from creation or appreciation of such emotions as, the 'Tragic' owes its genesis to the magic of the function of Suggestion, that converts the most ugly into the most charming, the extremely tiny into the strangely great, -- the strictly personal into the amazingly impersonal. It is the working of the function of Suggestion in the realm of poetry that differentiates the experience derived from other functions like Perception and Inference.

Since the theory adumbrated by neo-rhetorician is an extension of the theory propounded by Abhinavagupta in regard to genesis and appreciation of poetry, and since it has taken note of all the steps involved in the process of aesthetic presentation and aesthetic realisation, as proposed by representative literary critics, it may be interesting to analyse the steps involved in the process in the doctrine proposed by the neo-rhetorician. These steps in this doctrine are as follows:

(a)In a specimen of Poetic and Dramatic Art the literary artist and the trained actors exhibit the excitants and the ensuents, the permanent and the transient moods: the connoisseur becomes conscious of all these factors.

(b)Subsequently, through the operation of the function

of Suggestion the connoisseur locates the dominant mood of the specimen of literary art.

(c) At a later stage, as the mind of the refined reader gets itself concentrated on the dominant mood in the document of literary art, the special intellectual training obtained by him helps him in concentrating completely on the mood.

(d) When this complete concentration takes place, an error develops, as a result of which, the refined reader thinks himself identical with the original personage : as soon as this sense of identification creeps in his mind, an emotion is generated, as a result of which he derives supra-mundane delight.

(e) This emotion, therefore, is not real personal emotion belonging to the refined reader, but an artificial emotion comparable to the silver produced on the mother-o'-pearl generated due to some defect residing either in the subject or in object, or in the essential equipment.

(f) This generation of the artificial emotion is effected through the magical powers of the error or the defect, springing from the trained intellectual powers of the connoissuer : when this error or defect disappears, the artificial emotion also takes leave. In his effort to explain the process of aesthetic realisation without taking recourse to the new functions, as contemplated in the scheme of earlier theoreticians, the neo-rhetorician states that, the particular can never assume a universal form nor can the personal be raised to the status of the impersonal, unless the existence of an error or a defect is postulated. The particular is always the particular : the personal is sure to continue as personal for all time to come. It is only the operation of a defect, may be inherent in the poetic process, due to which the individual can appear as the general and the personal as the impersonal. Thus as postulation of an error becomes an essentiality, the neo-rhetorician says that, it is better to explain the sense of identification of the literary artist and the refined appreciator with the characters through the operation of this defect, rather than through postulation of certain new functions, as endorsed in the scheme of earlier literary theoreticians.[13]

The neo-rhetorician realises the danger to which the new theory is exposed. It is true that in case of identification of the literary artist and the responsive reader with the hero of a poem, depicting a pleasant emotion, unmixed bliss may be enjoyed ; but in case of their identification with the hero in the poem depicting the unpleasant mood what happens? The argument that the real emotion may lead to joy or sorrow as the case may be; but the artificial emotion always leads to bliss and bliss alone does not cut much ice, because such an assertion is likely to make the situation more confused, inasmuch as, the artificial snake produced on the rope does not generate unmixed bliss but causes the same feeling that is produced by the real snake.

The neo-rhetorician, however, does not hesitate to answer the set of questions: why does the literary critic, therefore, feel encouraged to produce the document of literary art? Why does the appreciative reader, in his turn, feel attracted towards the document, irrespective of the nature of emotion presented in it? In replying to these questions, he himself points out to the magic of the function of Suggestion, which, it is said, converts the unpleasant into the pleasant, – the trifling into sublime. This question anticipated by the neo-rhetorician itself shows that in his Theory, which is an extension of the earlier theories adumbrated by Indian Aesthetics 'Rasa' is experienced not by the appreciative connoisseur only, but by the literary artist as well, when he is engaged in carving out poetical paintings, competent to give expression to the artificial emotion generated in his mind. This theory, as recorded by Jagannatha, is a further improvement on the earlier theories, because while it recognises all these steps necessary for aesthetic presentation or aesthetic realisation, it pronounces for the first time in unequivocal terms the secret that 'Rasa' is experienced as much by the literary artist as by the refined reader, and consequently, emphatically observes that the emotion in poetry is an artificial one.

It is interesting that in his essay entitled *Tradition and the Individual Talent* T.S. Eliot acknowledges certain truths in his process of analysis of the 'poetic personality', - truths, which have been projected by Indian Literary Theory as well. Eliot believes that the literary artist is to use the ordinary emotion and to move from ordinary to extra-ordinary. It is not his business to find new emotions. Sanskrit Literary Theory enumerates certain permanent moods, which, as it says, belong to all persons of all ages and countries, and asserts that it is the duty of the literary artist to delineate one or the other of these permanent moods.[14] Eliot says that emotion presented in poetry is not the personal emotion of the poet; he may express feelings which are not actual emotions at all. This means that in the scheme of T.S. Eliot, the emotion presented in poetry cannot reach this impersonality unless the artist surrenders himself wholly to the work to be done. Sanskrit Literary Theory also says that the literary artist is required to transcend the limits of his small personality at the time of creation of poetry. With all emphasis at his command Eliot observes that poetry is not 'expression' of emotion, but rather an 'escape' from it. Sanskrit Literary Theory also says that, poetry is not an expression of personal emotion, but rather an escape from 'narrow personality'.

The efforts made by T.S. Eliot and the Sanskrit Literary Theory to draw a synthesis between the "expression" and the "escape" are amazingly similar. This does not mean, however, that T.S. Eliot obtained his data from Sanskrit Literary Theory. It only shows the profound influence exerted on him by the teachings of the Upanishads and the Gita. As the Sanskrit Literary Theory draws inspiration from the eternal truths preserved in the speculations of the Upanishads, the similarity between the theories propounded by the two appears as so great and significant. Eliot, however, has analysed mainly the process of creation of poetry, while Sanskrit Literary Theory has put greater emphasis on the process of poetic appreciation. But the two have moved frequently from one area to another, -- from the process of creation to the process of appreciation and from the process of appreciation again to the process of creation. As Sanskrit Literary Theory puts it : the two processes are not at poles asunder; rather they are complementary to each other: one cannot thrive without the other. To quote Abhinavagupta: the literary artist and the appreciative connoisseur conjointly constitute the essence of Poetic Art.[15]

REFERENCES

1. Poetry and Poetic Diction : William Wordsworth, p. 22 (*English Critical Essays: Nineeteenth Century,* Oxford University Press).
2. Ibid., p. 19-20.
3. Ibid., Appendx, pp. 27-32.
4. Tradition and the Individual Talent : T.S. Eliot, pp. 41 & 43 (*Selected Prose of T.S. Eliot,* Faber & Faber).
5. Ibid., pp. 43 & 44.
6. apūrvaṃ yadvastu prathayati vinā kāraṇakalāṃ
jagadgrāvaprakhyaṃ nijarasabharāt sārayati ca /
kramāt prakhyopākhyāprasarasubhagaṃ bhāsayati tat
sarasvatyāstattvaṃ kavisahṛdayākhyaṃ vijayatāt //
—*Locana* : Abhinavagupta, Maṅgala verse.
7. śabdārthaśaktyā vākṣipto vyaṅgyo'rthaḥ kavinā punaḥ /
yatrāviṣkriyate svoktyā sānyaivālaṃkṛtirdhvaneḥ //
— *Dhvanyāloka* : Ānandavardhana, II. 24
and
nīrasastu prabandho yaḥ so'paśabdaḥ mahān kaveḥ /
sa tenākavireva syādanyenāsmṛtalakṣaṇaḥ //
—Ibid., III. 19.
8. mukhyatayā duṣyantādigata eva raso ratyādiḥ kamanīya-vibhāvādyabhinayapradarśanakovide duṣyantādyanukartari naṭe samāropya sākṣātkriyate.
— *Rasagaṅgādhara* : Jagannātha, Chapter I, p. 123
(Chowkhamba Vidyabhavan Varanasi)
9. duṣyantādigato ratyādirnaṭe pakṣe duṣyantatvena gṛhīte
vibhādibhiḥ kṛtrimairapyakṛtrimatayā gṛhītaiḥ bhinne
viṣaye anumitisāmagryā balavatvādanumīyamāno rasaḥ.
—Ibid., p. 124.
10. tasmādabhidhayā niveditāḥ padārthā bhāvakatvavyāpāreṇāgamyātvādirasavirodhijñānapratibandhadvārā kāntātvādirasānukūladharmapuraskāreṇāvasthāpyante. evaṃ sādhāraṇīkṛteṣu duṣyanta-śakuntalā-deśa-kāla-vayo'vasthādiṣu paṅgau pūrvavyāpāramahimani, tṛtīyasya bhogakṛttvavyāpārasya mahimnā nigīrṇayo rajastamasorudriktasattvajanitena nijacitsvabhāvanirvṛti-viśrānti-lakṣaṇena sākṣātkāreṇa viṣayīkṛto bhāvanopanītaḥ sādhāraṇātmā ratyādiḥ sthāyī rasaḥ.
—Ibid., 98.

11. samucita-lalita-sanniveśacāruṇā kāvyena samarpitaiḥ sahṛdayahṛdayaṃ praviṣṭaiḥ tadīya-sahṛdayatāsahakṛtena bhāvanāviśeṣamahimnā viga'' taduṣyantaramaṇītvādibhira-laukikavibhāvānubhāva-vyabhicāriśabdavyapadeśyaiḥ śakuntalādibhirālambanakāraṇaiḥ candrikādibhiruddīpana- kāraṇaiḥ aśrupātādibhiḥ kāryaiḥ cintādibhiśca sahakāribhiḥ sambhūya prādurbhāvitena alaukikena vyāpāreṇa tatkāla-nirvartitānandāṃśāvaraṇājñānena ata eva pramuṣṭaparimita-pramātṛtvādinijadharmeṇa pramātrā svaprakāśatayā vāstavena nijasvarūpānandena saha gocarīkriyamāṇaḥ prāgviniviṣṭavāsanārūpo ratyādireva rasaḥ.

Ibid., 80.

12. apāre kāvyasaṃsāre kavireva prajāpatiḥ /
yathāsmai rocate viśvaṃ tathedaṃ parivartate //
śṛṅgārī cet kaviḥ kāvye jātaṃ rasamayaṃ jagat /
sa eva vītarāgaścet nirasaṃ sarvameva tat //

— *Dhvanyāloka* : Ānandavardhana, p. 238
(Nirnaya Sagar edn., Bombay).

13. navyāstu—'kāvye nāṭye ca kavinā naṭena ca prakāśiteṣu vibhāvādiṣu vyañjanavyāpāreṇa duṣyantādau śakuntalādiratau gṛhītāyāmanantaraṃ ca sahṛdayatollāsitasya bhāvanāviśeṣarūpasya doṣasya mahimā kalpitaduṣyantatvāvac- chādite svātmani ajñānāvacchinne, śuktikāsakala iva rajatakhaṇḍaḥ samutpadyamāno'nirvacanīyaḥ sākṣibhāsya-śakuntalā-tadviṣayaka-ratyādireva rasaḥ.

—*Rasagaṅgādhara* : Jagannātha, p. 101.
(Chowkhamba Vidyabhavan, Varanasi).

14. viruddhairaviruddhairvā bhāvairvicchidyate na yaḥ /
ātmabhāvaṃ nayatyāsu sa sthāyī lavaṇākaraḥ /
ciram citte'vatiṣṭhante sambadhyante' nubandibhiḥ
rasatavṃ ye prapadyante prasiddhāḥ sthāyino'tra te //

— *Rasagaṅgādhara* : Jagannātha, p. 127.
(Chowkhamba Vidyabhavan, Varanasi).

15. *Locana on Dhvanyāloka* : Abhinavagupta, p. 5 (Nirnaya Sagar edn., Bombay).

CHAPTER V

Utility of Poetry

Section I

Social Utility

It may be possible at this point of time to analyse the view of T.S. Eliot on the utility of poetry, particularly the fact as to whether the literary artist has got some direct social utility, and to examine whether Indian Aesthetics projects any of its views on this so-called utility of poetry. Eliot starts from the proposition that, the chief use of the meaning of a poem is 'to satisfy one habit of the reader, to keep his mind diverted and quiet, while the poem does its work upon him'. In this connexion, Eliot introduces the parallelism of 'a bit of nice meat' and says that, just as the house-dog is provided with this 'nice meat' by the imaginary burglar, similarly the reader is provided with pure pleasure by the literary artist; but the burglar has the deeper intention of committing a burglary, and in the same manner, the artist has a deeper intention of projecting certain truths through implementation of which a better social order can be ensured. While the literary artist is guided by the consideration of social utility, the reader is equally guided by a similar consideration of some tangible gain, apart from attainment of sane and wholesome pleasure. In the present century, Eliot asserts, nobody reads a whole poem for the purpose of pleasure alone: and this holds good more in case of 'long poems'. This does not, however, mean that a 'long poem' has become a thing of the past: what is emphasised is that, twentieth century readers are eager to trace more 'meanings' in them, — 'meanings', that are more practical and helpful. This naturally takes one to the gateway of controversial doctrine 'Art for Art's Sake' and its application in the realm of literary art, —the doctrine, in regard to which Eliot remarks: 'a mistaken one, and more advertised than practised'.[1]

The doctrine of "Art For Art's Sake" states that Poetic Art, nay, all art is intended to donate a sane and wholesome pleasure to the refined appreciator, as also to give an opportunity to the creative artist to give expression to his own self. The champions of this doctrine feel that poetic art, like all other arts, do not have a direct social utility, and that it does not render any material benefit to the society. It is not without reason, therefore, that the art of poetry had to meet a serious challenge from its opponents, who like Plato, affirm that the poets should be banished, because poetry conducts the reader to the dreamland of fancy, and makes him unable and unfit to face the hard realities of the external world of experience. In order to silence these critics of the art of poetry the champions of poetry had to expend considerable energy in analysing the benefits that are supposed to accrue from poetry. The doctrine of 'Art For Art's Sake', however, thinks that though poetry could have other minor utilities, the prime purpose served by it is induction of sane and wholesome pleasure, — impersonal and unmixed bliss, so to say, in the mind of both the artist and the appreciator. It is said that poetry serves this purpose by working on emotion, inasmuch as, it is the task of the art of poetry to transplant emotion from the mind of the creative artist to the mind of the appreciator. T.S. Eliot considers emotion as the essence of poetic art and affirms that, the only way of expressing emotion, in the form of art is by finding an 'objective correlative'. By 'objective correlative' he means a set of object, a chain of events, a series of characters and situations which could turn out to be the formula of the particular emotion intended to be expressed by the artist.[2] Though Eliot considers emotion as the centre of gravity of poetic art and recognises the necessity of finding an 'objective correlative' suitable for giving expression to this emotion, and though he accepts the view that, the chief objective of poetry is to cause emotive experience, and thereby to generate supra-mundane delight in the mind of the appreciator, he believes that poetry has some direct social utility as well. When Eliot says, "Every poet would like, I fancy, to be able to think that he had some direct social utility", he means that as no poet can feel quite sure of the permanent value of what he has written, it is better for him to have at least the satisfaction of having a part to play in the society. In explaining his view Eliot says that, it is not his intention to project the thought that the poet should meddle with "the tasks of the theologician, the preacher, the economist, the sociologist", because while other branches of learning are required to deal with "truth of fact", poetry is required to deal with "truth of probability". What Eliot means is that, while trying to transplant blissful experience from the mind of the artist to the mind of the connoisseur, poetry should also try to serve some social utility so that, the expectations of society can be fulfilled at least to some extent.[3]

It may be interesting to project the common points in the thought-currents of T.S. Eliot and some of the writers of Indian Aesthetics on the grand doctrine of 'Art For Art's Sake'. Indian theory considers emotive experience as the be-all and end-all of poetry, and while trying to analyse the creative process it states that poetry is a medium through which the self of the artist gives expression to the abundance of bliss, that constitutes a part and parcel of its own self. Indian theory which draws its inspiration from the speculations of the Upanishads tries to rest the doctrine of 'Art For Art's Sake' on the three aspects of the Absolute Reality, — the aspect of Being, the aspect of Knowing and the aspect of Expressing. While the first two aspects of the Absolute Reality to signify which the grand expression Brahman is used, fall under the domain of other branches of learning, the aspect of expression falls under the jurisdiction of all arts including the Art of Poetry. When the mind of the creative artist becomes full of transcendental joy he wants to give expression to it, and in course of this poetry is brought into being.

In analysing the appreciative process, also, Indian theory states that the first and foremost objective of poetry is to cause supra-mundane delight springing from attainment of aesthetic experience in the mind of connoisseur.[4] When the connoisseur derives this experience, his normal flow of thoughts concerning mundane possessions and dispossessions is put to a halt, as a result of which he is conducted to a higher plane. When the artist constructs poetical paintings and finds out 'objective correlatives', most appropriate to the expression of emotion intended to be communicated by him, he also rises above the ordinary level of experience and reaches a higher plane. As both the creative artist and the receptive reader reach a higher level of consciousness, it becomes possible for the one to savour the delight of the other and absorb his experience into his own self.

In his endeavour to explain this splendid process of transfer of universal emotion from one mind to another Tagore gives a beautiful analysis. He refers to an incantation pronounced during the marriage ritual, — the incantation which records a declaration by the father of the girl to donate his daughter to the bridegroom. Tagore says that, simple chanting of the incantation or expression of the pious wish to donate does not make the donation complete and perfect. In order to complete the circuit of donation it becomes necessary for the bridegroom to chant another incantation which is intended for the bride: in this the bridegroom prays that let the mind of the bride be transplanted in him and his mind be transplanted in the bride. When this transplantation takes place or in other words, the minds of both the bride and the bridegroom reach the same level, then and then only the act of donation becomes complete. By giving this illustration Tagore wants to emphasize the point that, for successful completion of the process of donation what is necessary is that the two parties to the donation should reach the same level of consciousness. This exactly happens in case of the art of poetry. The creative artist reaches a universal plane by putting into slumber his narrow sense of individuality ; the connoisseur also is conducted to the general plane by making docile the sense of fragmented individuality. As both float in higher level of consciousness far removed from the thoughts of mundane possessions and dispossessions, it becomes possible for the one to share the experience and consequently the delight of the other. When Indian Theory speaks of liberation as one of the prime objectives served by poetry, it possibly refers to this aspect of poetic art, — the aspect in which this art liberates the mind from ego-centric desires and takes both the creative artist and the reader to a grand general plane. Poetry does not liberate in the sense that, the world of reality is denied altogether, because poetry cannot thrive in a situation where reality is denied to the world. Denial of reality to the world is a situation ideal for thriving of philosophy, but not of poetry. Poetry liberates in the sense that, the current of ego-centric desires is put to a halt,— the surface of the lake becomes free of waves and steady; but behind the surface there exists a far deeper sympathy for the universe and humanity.[5]

Though Indian Theory regards induction of supreme and transcendental bliss as the prime purpose of poetry, it is conscious of the other benefits that are supposed to accrue from application to poetry. Indian theory is conscious of the fact that no artist would feel prompted to devote himself to the pursuit of this act unless some material incentives are given to him. It therefore says that, poetry leads to reputation as also to abundance of wealth. In citing examples, it refers to the case of Kalidasa, who acquired profound reputation through composition of poetical and dramatic creations and of one Dhavaka, who is believed to have composed three plays for the emperor Sri Harsa and dedicated them to his royal patron in exchange of substantial sum. These are, of course, personal benefits. But Indian theory is conscious of the social utility of poetry as well. It says that poetry tenders advice in the sweet and enchanting manner of the beloved, and when the pill of advice tendered by the art of poetry is swallowed by the reader, he does not have the feeling that, what is being donated is actually an advice to behave in a particular way. The grander the poem, the more appreciable is this aspect of social utility. As a matter of fact, no grand poetry can ignore this aspect, as is evident from the cases of the two great Indian Epics, the Ramayana and the Mahabharata. Indian theory itself says that the Ramayana tenders advice to the posterity to follow the virtuous way of life shown by Rama and to eschew the wrong path followed by Ravana. The Mahabharata equally advises posterity to choose peace and betterment of humanity in the confrontation between the two ideals represented by the right to property and the right to live peacefully in the world. Indian theory thus accommodates the doctrine of 'Art For Art's Sake', but at the same time it requires that poetry should have some direct social utility.[6]

When the views of T.S. Eliot on the tenability of the doctrine 'Art For Art's Sake' and those of some Indian literary theoreticians on the same topic are taken into account, one is delightfully surprised to trace the common points in the two thought-currents. The question of one influencing the other does not arise, — but these common points simply indicate that human thought is one, and that though separated by barriers of age and country, race and nationality human mind thinks in the same manner, and as time marches on it tries to find out new truths by resting its observations on the truths established by earlier theoreticians. T.S. Eliot's theories on problems relating to creation and appreciation of poetry, therefore, are extremely significant, but it is equally interesting that, the fundamental truth projected in them is the same as that projected by Indian theory.

Section II

Absolute Utility

It is interesting that though Eliot speaks of social utility of poetry and controverts the doctrine of 'Arts for Art's Sake' in the realm of poetry, he often refers to the absolute value of poetry, which is represented by attainment of pleasure in case of both the artist and the reader. The reader experiences pleasure, ensuing from attainment of Aesthetic Experience, and the artist derives pleasure being able to communicate his pleasurable experience. Poetry, Eliot says, is definitely a cultural entertainment, but 'if, beyond keeping the interest of a crowd of people for that length of time, the author can make a play, which is real poetry, so much the better'. In concluding his Essay entitled 'The use of Poetry and use of Criticism', Eliot says that, if poetry commemorates a public occasion or celebrates a festival or decorates a religious rite or amuses a crowd, it is so much the better. But poetry has the deeper purpose of generating aesthetic satisfaction by making the man aware of the truth that lies hidden in his own being. As Eliot says, 'It may make us from time to time a little more aware of the deeper unnamed feelings, which form the substratum of our being, to which we rarely penetrate, for our lives are mostly a constant evasion of ourselves, and an evasion of the visible and sensible world'.[7]

All this shows the oscillation of the mind of T.S. Eliot, who does not subscribe to the theory that, the prime purpose of poetry is to please, but moots the proposition that poetry has social relevance and social utility. At the same time, he says that, from time to time poetry makes the man aware of the truth that lies hidden in his being, and possibly throws the suggestion that poetry reveals the greatness inherent in the man, and unfolds the grandeur of his personality, thereby providing spiritual nourishment to him. This double stand of the great critic appears puzzling to the ordinary reader, but when the doctrine of Eliot is analysed with the help of the approach of Indian Aesthetics the riddle is solved, because Sanskrit Literary Theory also betrays this double stand, and asserts that while Poetry pleases and preaches one or the other truth, it serves the deeper purpose of revealing bliss associated with one's own being and thus of attaining supramundane delight.

Sanskrit Literary Theory is aware of the charges that are usually levelled against poetry. As a matter of fact, Rajasekhara cites three of these charges, and says that, study of poetry is to be eschewed, because it presents ideas that have no conformity to concepts prevalent in the ordinary world of existence, and it tenders bad counsel to man and leads him astray, and because it employs indecorous expressions and presents indecent meanings, stimulating, thereby, base propensities and passions in the man. In spite of all this poetry is eulogised in highest terms as the doorstep to emancipation and as leading to liberation, in addition to religious and material enrichment and satisfaction of hedonistic desires. Sanskrit Literary Theory asserts that though Poetry serves a number of purposes, including material enrichment, attainment of knowledge concerning codes of conduct, and good counsel, the crest-mark of all purposes is represented by attainment of instantaneous delight springing from experience of Rasa. When this Rasa is experienced knowledge of all other knowables is obliterated and what takes place is the ultimate transcendence of all mental states in an equipose known as Samvid-visranti.[8]

In its endeavour to analyse the mental states produced from perception of poetry, Anandavardhana arrives at three conditions: druti or melting of the heart, dipti or ignition of the mind and vikasa or blooming of the mind in which it expands and tries to trace the universe in the agent of which it serves as the apparatus. Dhananjaya however, speaks of four aspects of aesthetic attitude: vikasa or full-bloom of the mind, which happens in case of experience of the Erotic and the Comic, vistara or expansion of the mind, which takes place in case of appreciation of the Heroic and the Marvellous, Ksobha or repulsion of the mind, which occurs at the time of enjoyment of the Disgustful and the Frightful, and viksepa or agitation, which is generated at the time of savouring of the Furious and the Pathetic. This postulation of mental states, as made by Sanskrit Literary Theory is interesting from the standpoint of Psychology, since it includes categories like the ugly and the sublime alike and tries to arrive at the ultimate transcendence over all flow of thoughts concerning mundane possessions and dispossessions, — transcendence, that gives rise to the state of perfect mental equilibrium, known as Atma-visranti, or the rest of the self on the self. This pleasurable state of rest of the self on the self is signified by the term 'Rasa' in Sanskrit Literary Theory: when experience of this transcendental Rasa takes place, the ego-boundaries of the experiencer expand, as a result of which he traces his identity with the universe and discovers the truth of his being.[9]

The theory adumbrated by T.S. Eliot on the question of utility of poetry as also the doctrine propounded by Sanskrit Literary Theory on the issue reveal a double stand, inasmuch as, both say that Poetry serves some social utility and also that, Poetry makes the man conscious of the truth inherent in his own being. Of these two purposes that are served by Poetry the first constitutes the relative utility, while the second the absolute or the real one. It is this absolute utility that receives a full-bodied form in the Aesthetics of Sri Aurobindo and emerges as the grand concept of spiritual nourishment and upliftment.

REFERENCES

1. The Use of Poetry and the Use of Criticism : T.S. Eliot (*Selected Prose of T.S. Eliot* : Faber & Faber), pp. 93-94.
2. Hamlet : T.S. Eliot (*Selected Prose of T.S. Eliot* : Faber & Faber), p. 48.
3. The Use of Poetry and the Use of Criticism : T.S. Eliot (*Selected Prose of T.S. Eliot* : Faber & Faber), p. 95.
4. sakalaprayojanamaulibhūtaṃ rasāsvādanasamudbhūtaṃ vigalitavedyāntaramānandam ...

   — *Kāvyaprakāśa*, Chapter I, Vṛtti.
5. caturvargaphalaprāptiḥ sukhādalpadhiyāmapi /
   kāvyādeva yatastena tatsvarūpaṃ nigadyate //

   —*Sāhityadarpaṇa*, I. 2.
6. kāvyaṃ yaśase'rthakṛte vyavahāravide śivetarakṣataye /
   sadyaḥ paranirvṛtaye kāntāsammitatayopadeśayuje //

   — *Kāvyaprakāśa*, I. 2.
7. The Use of Poetry and the Use of Criticism : T.S. Eliot (*Selected Prose of T.S. Eliot* : Faber & Faber), p. 96.
8. asatyābhidheyatvānnopadeṣṭavyaṃ kāvyaṃ
   asadupadeśakatvāttarhi nopadeṣṭavyaṃ kāvyaṃ
   asabhyārthābhidheyatvānnopadeṣṭavyaṃ kāvyaṃ.

   — *Kāvyamīmāmsa*, G.O.S., pp. 24-26.
9. *Dhvanyāloka*, II. 9-12.

CHAPTER VI

Retrospect & Prospect

Section I

The Backward View

The discussions introduced in the foregoing chapters bring clearly into light the similarities between the thought-currents projected by T.S. Eliot in his critical essays and those floated by Sanskrit Literary Theories. These thoughts centre round some of the major problems relating to the creative as well as the appreciative process of Poetry. It is really amazing that though separated by centuries T.S. Eliot and some of the stalwarts in the field of ancient Indian literary criticism have expressed almost identical views and have viewed both the processes of creation and appreciation of poetry as very complex ones.

In his famous essay entitled 'Tradition and the Individual Talent' Eliot has opened his discussion with the observation that 'no poet, no artist of any art has his complete meaning alone', and has proceeded to observe that the poet is required to be aware of the mind of the nation, — a mind which is more important than his private mind, — because it is the experience of this mind of the nation that does not superannuate a really great poet. Sanskrit Literary Theory recognises this acquaintance with the mind of the nation as one of the essential requirements of the literary artist and tenders advice to budding poets to make themselves acquainted with specimens of great literarture produced in the soil, so that the spirit of the nation and the country can be reflected in the newly produced document of Art. While the mind of Europe has always kept itself engaged in the area of material and economic existence of man, the mind of India has concentrated itself on his spiritual existence, as a result of which there has been divergence in the ideals reflected in specimens of grand literature produced in two parts of the globe. And only those poems that have been able to provide nourishment to the spiritual existence of man and to project the greatness of the Infinite man lying behind the finite man have been accepted as specimens of Sublime Poetry according to Indian standards.

In the same essay T.S. Eliot has drawn a line of demarcation between the literary artist, the man and the literary artist, the creator and has proceeded to express the opinion that 'the more perfect the artist, the more completely separate in him will be the man who suffers and the mind which creates'. This means that, in his personal capacity the poet may experience an emotion, but when he gives expression to the emotion it becomes transmuted and is converted into a finer feeling. It is the magic of Art that transforms the raw emotion into a brilliant aesthetic mood enabling the reader to savour the delight associated with it. Sanskrit Literary Theory takes note of this conversion of brute emotion into a fine aesthetic mood and demonstrates the principle by making a referencae to the genesis of the Ramayana, — the first specimen of Literary Art. On listening to the pitiful lementations of the she-quail, when she gives vent to her grief at the death of her mate, Valmiki experiences the brute emotion of grief, but then it is transformed into the tragic and as it goes out in the external world it takes the shape of verse, — the Sloka. Indian Literary Theory considers the poet as a seer and envisages combination of two functions in him, — the function of realising the truth and the function of giving a graphic description of the truth realised. It is the profound imaginative faculty of the poet that enables him to realise the truth and carve out a poetical painting competent to give expression to the truth realised, and it is this imaginative faculty that transforms the raw or brute emotion into a fine aesthetic mood.

Eliot considers emotion as the centre of gravity of Poetic Art and in his endeavour to locate the machinery necessary for expressing emotion in the form of Art arrives at the concept of 'objective correlative'. In his Essay entitled 'Hamlet' Eliot says, "The only way of expressing emotion in the form of Art is by finding an 'objective correlative'"; and in explaining this concept further elaborates it as being represented by 'a set of objects, a situation, a chain of events, which shall be the formula of that particular emotion'. Sanskrit Literary Theory also considers suggested emotional mood as the soul of Poetry, and employs the term 'Rasa' to signify the state of blissful aesthetic experience. In its attempt to explain the formula for expression of the emotional mood, Sanskrit Poetics arrives at the concepts of Vibhava, Anubhava, Vyabhicaribhava and Sthayibhava, and formulates the doctrine according to which Rasa is to be implanted in poetry through presentation of the Vibhavas and the like, which are nothing but poetic representations of the set of objects, situations and chains of events. It is said that when characters and situations, set of objects and chains of events are represented through medium of expression in poetry, they acquire universal dimension and raise Rasa into comprehension through the function of suggestion. And Sanskrit Poetics proclaims Rasa as a state of beatitude in which the universalised subject of experience is confronted with the generalised object of experience.

While elaborating the nature of emotion, Eliot says that, the emotion expressed in poetry is not personal to the poet, that the emotion belongs to the poem and not to the poet, — and that an emotion which the artist has never experienced may serve his purpose as well as those familiar to him. Since the emotion is artificial, the contention of William Wordsworth that poetry is 'emotion recollected in tranquility', Eliot asserts, is not tenable. In his endeavour to substantiate his proposition Eliot explains that in Poetry there is neither real emotion nor recollection, and from this assertion arrives at the conclusion that 'Poetry is not a turning loose of emotion, but an escape from emotion; it is not the expression of personality, but an escape from personality'. Indian Literary Theory equally accepts this process of depersonalisation, and though applying it mainly in regard to the refined appreciator engaged in the process of experiencing poetry, points out its applicability in regard to the artist engaged in the process of construction of poetical paintings as well, and maintains that at the time of creation as well as appreciation of poetry the process of depersonalisation takes place, and both the poet and the connoisseur shun their sense of truncated ego and are conducted to a higher plane of consciousness. The question as to whether in a situation of total effacement of 'personality' poetry can be created and poetical paintings carved out naturally arises to make the paradox more confusing. To get out of the difficulties it is profitable to have a look at the theory projected by Tagore on this issue. Tagore envisages the existence of two types of ego, — the truncated ego and the expanded ego, and expresses the opinion that though the truncated ego is rendered docile at the time of creation of poetry, the workshop of the expanded ego is set in motion, as a result of which the specimen of Art produced reflects the universe in its small compass, enabling the reader to have an opportunity of experiencing the grand and the Infinite. Tagore employs the expression 'Individuality', to signify the 'small ego' and the term 'Personality' to refer to the 'expanded ego'. Poetry, therefore, is not an expression of truncated ego; it is an escape from Individuality.

In his critical essay, entitled 'The use of poetry and the use of Criticism' Eliot discusses the issue of utility of poetry and explains away the doctrine of 'Art for Art's Sake' as a mistaken theory, which is more advertised than practised. Poetry, he says, definitely pleases, but at the same time it has some direct social utility, and therefore, has to communicate some definite message. If apart from this communication it can blossom forth as real Poetry, catering to the needs of the aesthetic instinct lying latent in man so much the better. While concluding his essay Eliot again gives expression to his philosophical approach and maintains that, poetry makes the man aware of his deeper, unnamed feelings, which form the substratum of his being betraying thus his double stand in the matter of utility of Poetry. Strangely enough, Sanskrit Literary Theory speaks of six-fold purposes of Poetry, including material wellbeing, attainment of good counsel and experience of blessedness, springing from aesthetic realisation, but at the same breath says that, the crestmark of all purposes is represented by attainment of supramundane delight arising from experience of Rasa. In explaining this concept of Rasa, Sanskrit Theory projects the idea that it consists in manifestation of bliss, that constitutes a part and parcel of the man's being, and therefore, in repose of the soul in its own self. The contradiction, however, vanishes when material enrichment and other social purposes are accepted as constituting the relative utility in contradistinction to the revelation of the truth lying latent in the being of the man, that represents the absolute utility. This absolute utility receives recognition at the hands of Sri Aurobindo, who regards spiritual upliftment as the real purpose of Poetry.

Section II

Sri Aurobindo and the new Horizon

Since Sri Aurobindo is concerned mainly with spiritual poetry or mystic poetry, the type of which is represented by the brilliant document of Poetic Art, 'Savitri', his views on the problems of Aesthetics are naturally different from the views of ordinary thinkers. The views of Sri Aurobindo on some fundamental problems of Aesthetics are in a position to give a clear picture of the poetic process of creation as also of the process of appreciation of poetry in general.

Western Aesthetics floats the concept of Katharsis, and says that, poetry purges the mind of the base feelings of pity and horror, and places the reader on a higher level of consciousness, so that he can have the satisfaction of purification. Indian Aesthetics, however, starts from the idea of 'purified mind' of the appreciator, and in its endeavour to describe the refined appreciator to whom the document of Literary Art has its real appeal it introduces the concept of

'Sahridaya'. In explaining the 'Sahridaya', Sanskrit Literary Theory says that he represents a man of trained intellectual powers, — who makes himself acquainted with the specimens of Poetic Art, as a result of which whose mind becomes full of responsiveness to the characters and situations presented in Poetry. It is this man of trained intellectual powers to whom the document of Literary Art has its real appeal. Among the European literary critics T.S. Eliot is the only author who accepts the proposition that the appreciative reader should have 'sufficient brain-work', and should be full of responsiveness to the series of objects and chain of events, characters and situations, presented in poetry, so that the emotion expressed by the literary artist can be easily shared by him. Sri Aurobindo goes a step further, and in conformity to his Philosophical Doctrine that, evolution of man is a continuous process and that the transitional being man is to evolve from his present state to the state of supramental being starts from the point of refined spirit, and not from unpurified mind, as indicated by Western Aesthetics or purified mind, as projected by Indian Aesthetics and T.S Eliot, and at last arrives at the terminal point of real spiritual upliftment, where the man is able to reach the ideal of the superman.

Sri Aurobindo takes up the question as to whether Philosophy has got any place in Poetry at all. Finally, he expresses his opinion that, Philosophy has its place in Literary Art and it can even take a leading place along with psychological experience as it does in the Gita. All depends, however, on the manner of presentation. If it is dry, — a bare intellectual statement or an expression of a dead truth, it is philosophy; if, on the other hand, it is a living philosophy, presented in a beautiful manner so much so that, the truth presented becomes capable of remaining dynamic in the spirit of the man, then it blossomes forth into the rose of Poetry. In his attempt to controvert the charges of unintelligibility brought against 'Savitri', Sri Aurobindo says that the case is so, because the truth expressed in it is unfamiliar to the ordinary minds or belongs to an untrodden domain or enter into a field of occult experience, and not because there is any attempt to present a dark or vague thought. The thinking is not intellectual, but intuitive or more than intuitive, always causing a vision and spiritual contact or a knowledge which has come by entering into the thing itself by identity.

Sri Aurobindo, thus, justifies the right of the poet to philosophise in poetry and declares that the poet has definitely got the right to think as well as to see and feel. He agrees with the modernists in their revolt against the objection to thinking and philosophical reflection in poetry as projected by the romantist. But he does not go too far as the modernists do. The modernists try to turn emotion out of the intimate chamber of the house of poetry and in their endeavour to avoid rhetorical writing and beauty of style talk of loading poetry too much with dry and exaggerated thought. Sri Aurobindo does not think that emotion should be turned out of the inner chamber of poetry nor that poetry should be loaded too much with exaggerated thoughts.

Sri Aurobindo does not regard poetry as an expression of the personality of the poet, because the personality of the literary artist is to be rendered completely docile by surrendering itself at the altar of the Divine being. The artist of the sublime poetry, Sri Aurobindo thinks, is to start from the sense of absolute surrender, because it is complete surrender alone that can bring down the grace of the Divine being. And when God grows in man and the waters of his being are permeated by the rays of God, even little amount of effort produces biggest of the results. This exactly happens in case of Sublime Poetry; when the grace of the Divine being flows Inspiration starts working at a high level, and thoughts and emotions, expressions and contents, metres and figures automatically rush forth, building thereby a brilliant poetic texture. In the Philosophy of Sri Aurobindo man is more a spiritual being striving after the status of a supramental spirit, and consequently the weak personality of the man, having material or economic existence alone does not have any place in his scheme. Sri Aurobindo, therefore, accepts poetry as a total escape from personality, because it is 'Inspiration' working at a higher level through Divine grace that carves out poetical paintings, and not the imagination of the poet working at an ordinary level.

Coming to the question of utility of poetry, Sri Aurobindo points out only to the absolute utility represented by spiritual upliftment. Man is a transitional being moving from the state of animalhood to the state of supermanhood and in his journey to this supermanhood or the state of "Supramental spirit" Poetry is to render assistance to him by bringing out the spiritual possibilities lying latent in man. Sri Aurobindo, therefore, does not conceive of poetry as an instrument leading to fame or material prosperity or knowledge concerning the ways of life, but envisages it only as a means of effecting spiritual upliftment. The clarion call issued to posterity by Sri Aurobindo is that, the waters of the spirit should be poured into the physical mould, so that this transient human body could be utilised for the purpose of attaining immortality and in this process of attainment of immortality and emergence as a 'Superman' Poetry has its role to play.

Sri Aurobindo does not accept the Theory of 'Art for Art's Sake', because as he says, acceptance of this theory is likely to render Poetry a trifling means of cultural entertainment and amusement of the civilised mind. Poetry is not simply a cultural entertainment: it is to lead to spiritual upliftment at the ultimate level, and consequently, it is more than a means for attainment of Aesthetic Realisation (Rasa), as is described by general Sanskrit Literary Theory. Sri Aurobindo, therefore, floats the idea of the 'Overmind Poetry', and continues to say that the Overmind and Aesthetic cannot be equated together. Aestheticism is concerned mainly with Beauty, but more with Rasa, —the repose of the mind on the vital feeling, but this may not necessarily be a spiritual feeling. Aesthetics belongs to the mental range and depends upon it. The Overmind is essentially a spiritual power. Mind in it surpasses its ordinary self and takes its stand on a spiritual foundation. It embrace beauty and sublime: it sees universal and eternal beauty, while it takes up and transforms all that is limited and broad. It is concerned specially with truth and knowledge or rather with wisdom that exceeds knowledge; it is truth that goes beyond the truth of fact and truth of thought. It has the truth of spiritual thought and spiritual feeling, and ultimately truth and beauty go together and coincide. Sri Aurobindo feels that when the Overmind speaks through poetry it puts truth first and does not consider the limited Aesthetics as its purpose. 'Overmind Poetry', thus, as Sri Aurobindo envisages, is a means leading to spiritual upliftment; it does not remain content with presentation of Aesthetic relish alone: it works in the inner spirit of the man and makes the truth dynamic in the soul, as a result of which, what is experienced is not a simple passionate emotion, but a spiritual transcendence and equilibrium. This 'Overmind Poetry' as Sri Aurobindo declares, is a gift of inspiration, which presents not only the feeling and the thought, but carves out poetical paintings, as well, competent to give expression to the spiritual truth visualised.

Sri Aurobindo,.thus, moves further from the terminal point arrived at by Indian Aesthetics and goes deeper into the inner spirit of the man, and formulates principles of literary adjudication by considering the reaction produced by the document of literary art not on the mind of the appreciator, — his lower vital and sensational reaction, but by taking into account the reaction produced on the spirit. The business of the critical intellect is to appreciate and judge: in the case of 'Overmind Poetry' it is the business of the intellect to adjudicate; but the difficulty is posed by the problem of laying down rules for adjudication of 'Overmind Poetry'. While, in the case of normal poetry, principles can be easily formulated, because the flow of imagination has a course of its own, in case of 'Overmind Poetry' the situation is different, since overhead inspiration does not follow a definite course and 'there is always the risk of this overhead inspiration stepping across the wall and passing on leaving the critical initellect bewildered and at a loss to understand'. The mere critical intellect not touched by rare sight can do little here. Only those who are initiated into the mystery of 'Overmind Poetry' are in a position to catch the thought-element projected in it and appreciate its beauty, or in other words, a sufficient 'brain-work' is necessary to enter into the secret of this type of poetry and this brain-work ultimately depends on the grace of God, which donates the third eye to the appreciator, enabling him to understand the implication of the mystic poetry and catch the charmingness of the overmind literary creation. After all, as Sri Aurobindo asserts, man is not a fixed being: he is a transitional one and his movement is to be conducted from manhood to supermanhood, —from the mental man to the state of supramental being. The 'Overmind' reveals its mysteries only to that man, who is aspiring after supermanhood and is striving for transformation from the mental state to the supramental one; and at the same time, it serves as an equipment for this transformation. Poetry, therefore, is not simply a cultural entertainment; it is a *Purnayoga*.

BIBLIOGRAPHY

Works by T.S. Eliot, Faber, unless otherwise stated.

Prufrock and Other observations. The Egotist, London, 1917.

Ezra Pound, His Metric and His Poetry. Alfred A. Knopf, New York, 1918.

Poems. The Hogarth Press, London, 1919.

Ara Vos Prec. The Ovid Press, London, 1920.

Poems. Alfred A. Knopf, New York, 1920.

The Sacred Wood. Methuen, London. 1920.

The Waste Land. Boni and Liveright, New York, 1922.

The Hogarth Press. London, 1923.

Homage to John Dryden. The Hogarth Press. London, 1924.

Poems, 1909-1925, 1925.

For Lancelot Andrewes, 1928.

Dante, 1929.

Ash-Wednesday, 1930.

Anabasis, A Poem by St. J. Perse with translation by T.S. Eliot, 1930.

Thoughts After Lambeth, 1931.

Triumphal March, 1931.

Selected Essays, 1932.

John Dryden : The Poet, the Dramatist, the Critic. Terence & Elsa Holiday, New York, 1932.

Sweeney Agonistes, 1932.

The Use of Poetry and the Use of Criticism, 1933.

After Strange Gods, 1934.

The Rock, 1934.

Elizabethan Essays, 1934.

Murder in the Cathedral, 1935.

Essays Ancient and Modern, 1935.

Collected Poems, 1909-1935, 1936.

The Family Reunion, 1939.

Old Possum's Book of Practical Cats, 1939.

The Idea of a Christian Society, 1939.

East Coker, 1940.

Burnt Norton, 1941.

The Dry Salvages, 1941.

Little Gidding, 1942.

Four Quartets, 1944.

Notes Towards the Definition of Culture, 1948.

The Cocktail Party, 1950.

The Complete Poems and Plays, 1909-1950, 1952.

The Confidential Clerk, 1954.

On Poetry and Poets, 1957.

The Elder Statesman, 1959.

Collected Plays, 1962.

George Herbert. *Writers and Their Work*, Longmans, Green & Co., Harlow, 1962.

Collected Poems, 1909-1962, 1963.

Knowledge and Experience in the Philosophy of F.H. Bradley, 1964.

To Criticize the Critic, and other writings, 1965.

Poems Written in Early Youth, 1967.

The Complete Poems and Plays of T.S. Eliot, 1969.

Selected Prose of T.S. Eliot (ed.) Frank Kermode, 1975.

Biography

Tate, Alan (ed.), *T.S. Eliot : The Man and his Work*. Chatto & Windus, London, 1967.

Gordon, Lyndall, *Eliot's Early Years*. Oxford University Press, Oxford, 1977.

Behr, Caroline. *T.S. Eliot: A Chronology of his Life and Work*. Macmillan. London, 1983.

Ackroyd, Peter., *T.S. Eliot*. Hamish Hamilton, London, 1984.

Gordon, Lyndall, *Eliot's New Life*. Oxford University Press. Oxford, 1988.

Criticism

Leavis, F.R. New Bearings in English Poetry. Chatto & Windus, London, 1932.

Matthiessen, F.O., *The Achievement of T.S. Eliot*. Oxford University Press. London, 1935, rev. ed. 1947.

Preston, Raymond, *'Four Quartets'*. Rehearsed. Sheed & Ward, New York, 1946.

Gardener, Helen, *The Art of T.S. Eliot*. Cresset Press, London, 1949.

Bradbrook, M.C., *T.S. Eliot, Writers and Their Work*. Longmans, Green & Co. London, 1950; rev. ed. 1965.

Williamson, George, *A Reader's Guide to T.S. Eliot*. Thames & Hudson. London, 1955.

Braybrooke, Neville (ed.), *T.S. Eliot: A Symposium*. Hart-Davis, London, 1958.

Kenner, Hugh, *The Invisible Poet*. W.H. Allen, London, 1960.

Smidt, Kristian, *Poetry and Belief in the Work of T.S. Eliot*. Routledge & Kegan Paul, London, 1961.

Stead, C.K., *The New Poetic: Yeats to Eliot*. Penguin, London, 1964.

Hirai, Masao and Tomlin, E.M.F. (eds.), *T.S. Eliot: A Tribute from Japan*. Kenkyusha, Tokyo, 1966.

Southam, B.C., *The Student's Guide to the Selected Poems of T.S. Eliot*. Faber, London, 1968.

Browne, E. Martin, *The Making of T.S. Eliot's Plays*. Cambridge University Press. London, 1969.

Bantock, G.H., *T.S. Eliot and Education*. Faber, London, 1970.

Eliot, Valerie (ed.), *The Waste Land:* a facsimile and transcript of the original drafts. Faber, London, 1971.

Bergonzi, Bernard, *T.S. Eliot*. Macmillan, London, 1972.

Leavis, F.R., *The Living Principle:* English as a Discipline of Thought. Chatto & Windus, London, 1975.

Traversi, Derek, *T.S. Eliot: The Longer Poems*. Bodley Head, London, 1976.

Moody, A.D., *Thomas Stearns Eliot: Poet*. Cambridge University Press, Cambridge, 1979.

Grant, Michael (ed.), *T.S. Eliot: Poet and Critic.* New Pelican Guide to English Literature, Vol. 7, Penguin, London, 1983.

Hinchcliffe, Arnold P. (ed.), *T.S. Eliot: Plays* - A Selection of Critical Essays. Macmillan, London, 1985.

Ricks, Christopher, *T.S. Eliot and Prejudice.* Faber, London, 1988.

Scofield, Martin, *T.S. Eliot: The Poems.* Cambridge University Press, Cambridge, 1988.

Mitra, Sourin, *T.S. Eliot: the Critic,* D.K. Publishers Distributors (P) Ltd., Delhi.

Sen, M.K., *Inter-War English Poetry,* The University of Burdwan, 1967.

Lu, Fei-Pai., *T.S. Eliot: The Dialectical Structure,* The University of Chicago, 1966.

Sarkar, Subhas, *Eliot & Yeats: A study,* The Minerva, 1978.

Sarkar, Subhas, *T.S. Eliot the Dramatist,* The Minerva, 1972.

A. Hauser, *The Social History of Art.*

B. Bosanquet, *A History of Aesthetics.*

S. Langer, *Feeling and Form.*

C. Ogden & I.A. Richards, *The Meaning of Meaning.*

H. Read, *Art and Society.*

G. Santayana, *The Sense of Beauty.*

R. Wallek, *A History of Modern Criticism,* 4 Vols.

M. Weity, *Problems of Aesthetics.*

L. Wittgenstein, *Lectures and Conversations on Aesthetics.*

B. Croce, *Aesthetic.*

M.C. Beardsley, *Aesthetics From Classical Greece to the Present.*

R. Fry. *Vision and Design.*

Anandavardhana, *Dhvanyaloka.*

Jagannatha, *Rasagangadhara.*

Kuntaka, *Vokroktijivita.*

Rajasekhara, *Kavyamimamsa.*

Mammata, *Kavyaprakasa.*

Abhinavagupta, *Locana.*

K. Krishnamoorthy, *Abhinavagupta Dhvanyaloka-Locana,* Meharchand Lachhmandas Publications, 1988.

K. Krishnamoorthy, *Indian Literary Theories,* Meharchand Lachhmandas Publications, 1985.

K. Krishnamoorthy, *Studies in Indian Aesthetics and Criticism,* 1979.

R.R. Mukherji, *Literary Criticism in Ancient India,* Sanskrit Pustak Bhandar, Calcutta.

S.K. De, *Sanskrit Poetics* Firma KLM Pvt. Ltd.

J.L. Masson & M.V. Patwardhan, *Santarasa & Abhinavagupta's Philosophy of Aesthetics,* Bhandarkar Oriental Research Institute, Poona.

Letters

The Letters of T.S. Eliot, Vol. I: 1898-1922 (ed.) Valerie Eliot. Faber, London, 1988.

The Letters of T.S. Eliot, Vol. II: 1923-7 (ed.) Valerie Eliot. Faber, London, forthcoming.